Doll Collecting for Fun & Profit

by Mildred and Colleen Seeley

ABOUT THE AUTHORS

Mildred Seeley is well-known in the doll world. She is a doll maker and collector, and has been involved with dolls all her life.

An active member of the United Federation of Doll Collectors, Mildred has worked hard to get people all over the world interested in collecting dolls. She founded the Doll Artisan Guild, an organization for reproduction-doll makers.

Mildred is affectionately called the "First Lady Of Dolls," a title bestowed upon her by the International Ceramic Association and Expo Enterprises. She was given this recognition in 1982 at the California Doll Convention.

Always interested in telling the public about dolls, Mildred founded and edited for a number of years *The Dollmaker* magazine. She was also the founder and special editor of the *Doll Artisan* magazine, published by the Doll Artisan Guild.

Mildred's appreciation of dolls is heightened by her appreciation of art. She holds a bachelor's degree in art, and has studied sculpture and painting.

Colleen Seeley is Mildred's daughter. She has been collecting dolls since she was old enough to walk. During her childhood, Colleen received a handmade doll from her mother on every birthday. She soon became interested in making dolls herself.

At the age of 11, Colleen started making and selling folk dolls. For almost 12 years, she made and sold her handcrafted wood dolls to museums and gift shops.

Colleen's professional background is in communication arts. During high school, she edited an international magazine for youth. After college, she set up a freelance communications business, writing and editing publications for non-profit organizations.

Although she lives away from her family, Colleen still enjoys her dolls and tries to keep up with what's happening in the doll world. Writing this book with her mother was a project of love and sharing fond memories.

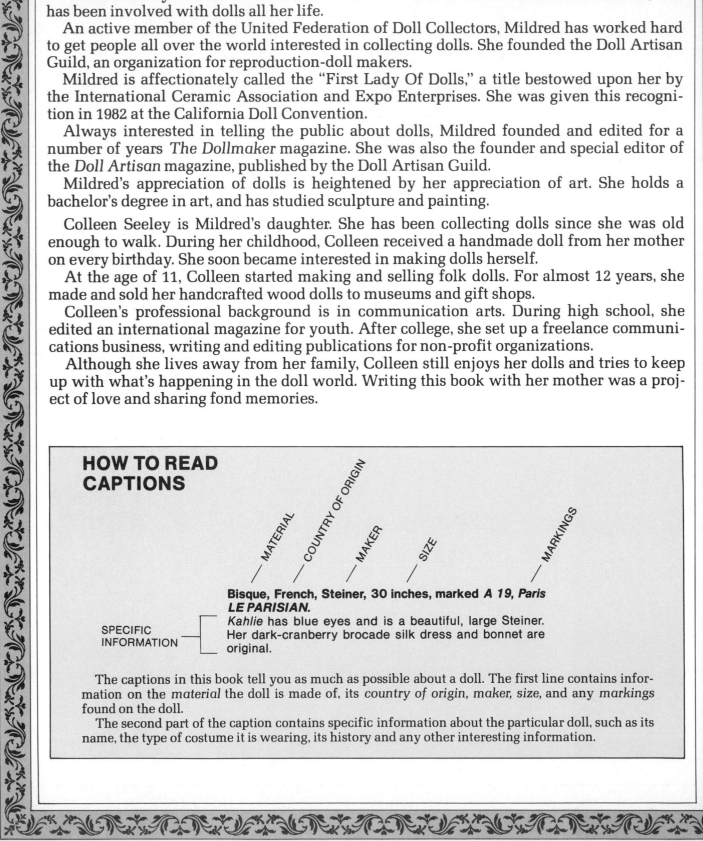

HOW TO READ CAPTIONS

MATERIAL   COUNTRY OF ORIGIN   MAKER   SIZE   MARKINGS

Bisque, French, Steiner, 30 inches, marked *A 19, Paris LE PARISIAN.*
Kahlie has blue eyes and is a beautiful, large Steiner. Her dark-cranberry brocade silk dress and bonnet are original.

SPECIFIC INFORMATION

The captions in this book tell you as much as possible about a doll. The first line contains information on the *material* the doll is made of, its *country of origin*, *maker*, *size*, and any *markings* found on the doll.

The second part of the caption contains specific information about the particular doll, such as its name, the type of costume it is wearing, its history and any other interesting information.

Table of Contents

Publishers: Bill and Helen Fisher; Executive Editor: Rick Bailey; Editorial Director: Randy Summerlin; Editor: Judith Schuler; Art Director: Don Burton; Book Design: Dana Martin; Major Photography: Mildred Seeley; Cover Photography: Ray Manley Studios.

HPBooks

P.O. Box 5367 Tucson, AZ 85703 (602) 888-2150
ISBN: 0-89586-207-7
Library of Congress Catalog Card Number: 82-84016
© 1983 Fisher Publishing, Inc. Printed in U.S.A.

ACKNOWLEDGMENT
Without Vernon Seeley's help and effort, we could not have completed our work. His continuing support made this book possible.

PHOTOGRAPHY NOTE
Dolls photographed for this book are from the authors' collection. The one exception is noted.

Starting a Doll Collection

A doll is a child's toy, but old dolls are more than toys. They are valuable pieces of history and art made many years ago.

Dolls were made as toys for children to love. Now, collectors love them and seek them for their own.

The dolls most often sought by collectors are old bisque dolls, made in France or Germany in the late 19th and early 20th centuries. *Bisque* is a form of porcelain clay, similar to the material in a fine dish but without the glaze. Most fine dolls are made of bisque. They are the most beautiful and rarest dolls available.

Dolls with special workmanship, charm and beauty are sought for all kinds of collections. Like other art pieces, dolls have interesting combinations of color, texture, shape and line. Years ago, when antique dealers piled dolls like cordwood, buyers had to sort them out. Now, with fewer dolls to meet demand, each doll is a prize.

Many fine old dolls are still available. Some are acquired for the sake of beauty and the joy of collecting. But more and more are collected for investment purposes. They are carefully bought with the expectation that they will increase in value.

INFORMATION TO HELP YOU

Dolls made of bisque are the most common to collect. Cloth, felt, china, wax and wood dolls are also popular with collectors.

Regardless of what others collect, it's impor-

Bisque, French, Jumeau, 32 inches, Long-Face Jumeau, marked *15*.
The doll at left has applied ears. The ball for the knee is attached to the upper leg. Her hair is coarse and she is wearing a child's old white dress. This is an example of a doll with universal appeal.

The picture at top is a close-up of the doll at left. Many people want a Long-Face Jumeau. The larger ones are the most appealing. This is the largest size known. Part of this doll's charm is its deep-blue paperweight eyes.

**Bisque, French, Steiner, 30 inches, marked *A 19*,
*Paris LE PARISIAN.***
Kahlie has blue eyes and is a beautiful, large Steiner. Her
dark-cranberry brocade silk dress and bonnet are original.

tant to develop your own appreciation of dolls. You should buy what *you* like. To protect your investment, you must know what you are looking for. This book shows you how to find and identify dolls, and how to select and judge prices. Knowledge of dolls and ways to collect can help you have a more enjoyable and valuable collection.

You will find detailed descriptions of dolls in this book. Doll collectors sometimes won't allow you to undress, remove the wig or take apart a doll to view its structure. We have done this for you in pictures to help you learn about dolls.

The prices included in this book are as up-to-date as possible at the time of publication.

Prices listed for a doll are an indication of what was paid at a specific time. Use prices to give you an idea of how values have changed for one doll. They also give you an idea of how prices vary from one doll to another. Use each *only* as a guide for choosing a doll, not as an absolute measure of today's worth.

There are three classifications of dolls—*moderns*, *collectables* and *antiques*. Moderns are dolls less than 25 years old. Collectables are dolls between 25 and 75 years old. Antiques are over 75 years old.

There are three types of collectors. The beginning collector is someone who has collected dolls for less than two years. The established col-

Bisque, French, marked *Paris H.G. 11.*
A rare doll, little is known about her.

lector has collected for 8 to 10 years. The lifetime collector has collected since childhood. The material provided and advice given in this book are for all three collecting levels.

COLLECTING IS AN ART

A collector should have a plan. Doll collecting shouldn't be a haphazard acquisition of any or all available dolls. It must be carefully planned and carried out. A person must decide what kind of dolls to collect and the amount of money to spend in finding and buying quality dolls. This is the *art* of doll collecting.

There are other factors that make doll collecting enjoyable. Knowledge about the subject increases your enjoyment. Knowing doll etiquette can help you have fun.

What You Need To Learn—Learn about dolls by studying the glossary in this book. Read everything you can about them. When people mention fashion dolls, character dolls, body types or style of heads, you will understand what they mean. Learn the language of the doll seller, the doll maker and the auction house. Knowing doll language can help you get started.

Study dolls using every available resource. But don't believe everything you read. What is *between* the lines is sometimes more important than what is written.

Bisque, French, Bru, marked *Bru Jne 11*.
Ask for permission to undress a doll down to her body before purchasing it. This Bru was a great find with her original underclothing, including a corset.

DOLL ETIQUETTE

Doll etiquette makes collecting enjoyable. It allows beginners to enter the doll world with confidence. By practicing etiquette, a beginner can relax, buy a doll and enjoy it. Knowing doll etiquette saves a collector embarrassment and gives a feeling of assurance. Follow these rules of doll etiquette:

1. Don't ask friends to go along when you are invited to see someone's dolls. Viewing a collection is an honor, so treat it this way. Enjoy the dolls and compliment your hostess on ones you enjoy. When you leave, don't quote prices, numbers or makers.

2. Never touch another person's dolls. Don't pick up a doll, examine its body or play with its hair. Don't bring children or animals into a home with a doll collection.

3. Always call in advance to arrange a visit with a collector. Some collectors have a problem with people who stop by unannounced. This happens to us because we live in an area where they come from all over the country. When people come to our home, we tell them we don't have our dolls on exhibit. We don't enjoy doing this, but it's necessary.

4. If you are a guest in a collector's home, don't photograph the dolls. If owners want their collections publicized, they will arrange to have them photographed.

5. When writing an article about someone's dolls, rules of etiquette apply. After obtaining permission for an article, let the collector read the article before submitting it to a publisher. Most people dislike articles written about them and their collection because articles often include mistakes, photographs or prices of dolls. Always ask before writing about a person's doll collection.

6. When attending a doll show, if you're interested in purchasing a doll, ask an attendant to help you. Don't be unreasonable. Decide by looking if you're interested. Don't touch. It's acceptable to ask to look underneath the clothes. You are not the only customer, so don't ask someone to hold a doll unless you intend to buy it. Don't ask for a discount unless you are a dealer with a tax number.

7. When you visit a dealer's shop, don't bring children or relatives with you. Ask the owner to undress ' *only* the dolls you are interested in buying. Call ahead if you wish to see a particular doll so the dealer will have it out.

8. At auctions, try to see everything possible in a limited time. Try not to block the view of other prospective buyers. It is acceptable to look and listen while a helper is showing a doll to someone else. This saves everyone time.

9. When buying from a dealer who sells dolls through the mail, send your money immediately. Return a doll promptly if it is not acceptable. Let the dealer know why you are not satisfied. You are not obligated to purchase a doll if you don't like it. Dolls should be *exactly* as described. If they aren't, this is reason enough to return it. You won't usually run into difficulty with an established dealer if you want to return a doll. If you owe shipping charges, pay them.

Dealers have rights, too. Return the doll in the condition you receive it. Don't remove or change anything. Pack the doll as it was packed and ship it promptly.

Bisque, French, Huret.
Huret dolls are valuable collectors' dolls because only a few were made. Most Huret dolls have unusual faces. The doll on the left has blond hair and paperweight eyes.

Markings on dolls are usually found on the back of the head and neck. Markings are like an artist's signature—they are the best clue to identifying a doll.

RECOGNIZING A COLLECTOR'S DOLL

There are qualities that make a doll a *collector's doll*. Dolls that are singled out at auctions and bring high prices by collectors are examples. Prize dolls usually have a combination of the following qualities.

Beauty—A beautiful doll is an object of joy. If a doll is beautiful, it is valuable.

Mark Of Identification—This important mark can add value to the doll. Like a painting, the signature or mark of the maker can add value.

Workmanship—Bisque dolls should be smooth,

with fine details such as brows, lashes and setting of eyes. Many people prefer dolls with the sparkling depth of paperweight eyes. *Paperweight eyes* have a glass bulge on the outside, giving depth to the eye. The doll's proportions must also be correct.

Rarity—If there is a large number of a particular doll, its value will not be high. If only a few dolls were made, that doll will be in demand. It will probably command a higher price.

Condition—Carefully check the condition of the doll. It should have no cracks, breaks or sub-

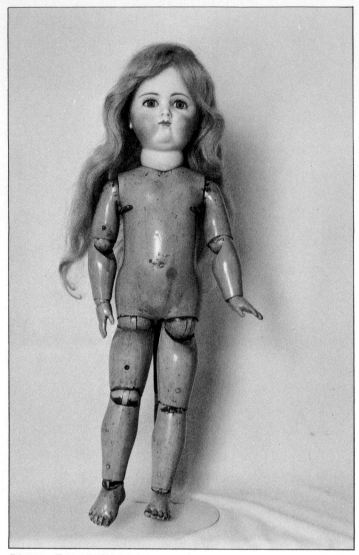

Bisque, French, Huret.
The Huret doll shows her jointed body and metal hands. She is an excellent doll for collection.

Bisque, French, Huret, 17-1/2 inches.
This doll has a jointed wooden body, with joints at the ankles and wrists. She has a stem of porcelain from her neck down into her body. Her platinum wig is of unknown material. The costume, including the bonnet, is original.

stituted parts. The doll should have its original wig in acceptable condition. Original eyes are also important. It's an added bonus to find a completely original costume with original, marked shoes. Many times a collector must accept a substitute costume of the correct size and style. Any costume should be attractive on the doll.

Uniqueness—Sometimes a doll's uniqueness becomes important. You must be careful because uniqueness is occasionally "created" by the seller. The doll's place in a collection may also make it valuable to a particular collector. Take care deciding if a doll is worth the price being asked. When the right doll comes along—one you've been hunting for or one to complete a series—be prepared to pay more. You may also have to wait patiently until the owner wants to sell.

Caution: Don't become obsessed with perfection in dolls. If you do, the joy of collecting is lost. Most dolls are not perfect. Hope for nearly perfect.

BEGINNING A DOLL COLLECTION

Doll collecting can be done at any age—from 8 to 98. It can be carried on to any degree. Five dolls normally make a collection. A doll can be valued from a few dollars to thousands of dollars. The collector's age, the number of dolls and the value do not matter. Doll collecting is fun!

Bisque, French, Bru, 18 inches, marked *Bru Jne 6.*
Comfort has a leather body, legs and feet. Her arms are leather, with the bisque hand inserted just above the wrist. This is a choice doll in the Seeley collection.

Doll collecting is a hobby you can start and stop. You can stop for years, then begin again. Even if you are not actively collecting, your investment accumulates value. Doll collecting can be enjoyed alone or shared with friends, at clubs, conventions and shows.

As you begin collecting, do your homework. Read as many books on dolls as you can. Use price guides. Study dolls at auctions and in auction catalogs. Develop your own judgment and taste. No one can know exactly what you want or how much you should pay. You must make your own decisions. Everyone makes mistakes, but mistakes can help you learn.

If you have no dolls and wish to start a collec-tion, check with your relatives. You'll be surprised how many have old dolls. They may be glad to have a member of the family care for family treasures. At least 15 of our dolls came from members of my family or my husband's. Family members may also help you locate dolls.

Many beginning collectors consult someone about purchasing a doll. Think twice before talking it over with anyone. Don't confide in auctioneers. They are interested in selling dolls for as high a price as possible. Don't consult with dealers who make their living selling dolls. Don't ask people in a doll club. Someone else may purchase the doll before you make up your mind.

Bisque, German, Kestner, 16 inches, marked *JDK 221*.
We named this doll *Dear Googly*. Googly-eye dolls are popular.

At an auction, don't talk to your best friend if she is planning to bid on the same doll. Don't get friendly with a person at an auction and offer not to bid on a doll so that person won't bid on a doll of your choice. Keep your intentions to yourself.

Sometimes a beginner can't decide about buying a doll. That was the case with one of our dolls, which we named *Dear Googly*.

In 1971, we were traveling through New Mexico on our way to Arizona. We stopped at an antique shop in Deming where the owner had a few dolls. After some discussion, she went into her house and brought out a Googly JDK 221 for us to see. It had a broken finger and the eyes would not close when she was laid back to sleep. My husband wanted the doll, but we didn't have $900 to buy her. We left, still think-ing about buying the doll he wanted so much.

When we got to Arizona, we decided we had to have the doll. We called the lady in New Mexico, told her we wanted the doll and offered to send a down payment. We couldn't pick up the doll until our return trip to New York a few weeks later.

The owner promised to keep the doll for us until we returned. We worried about it the rest of the time we were in Arizona, but the doll was there when we went back. We named the doll *Dear Googly*, because she was so expensive.

In 1979, we sold the doll for $2,400. We looked for a replacement and finally bought one for $3,200 in 1981. At the time we purchased our first Googly, it was our most expensive doll. Sometimes you have to take a chance and buy a doll when you have the opportunity.

Bisque, French, probably Lemoges, 18 inches.
This doll has top and bottom rows of teeth.

Her antique clothing and boots and bright-blue paperweight eyes make this doll attractive. Have a few unusual dolls in your collection. Too many unmarked dolls in a collection is not advisable.

QUALITIES OF A GOOD COLLECTION

A collection must be made up of dolls that last. They should stand the test of time. Dolls are sometimes collected for their beauty, like works of art. In some cases, they are collected because of a special interest. They may be collected for historical value. Most large, valuable collections have more than one theme, group or type of doll.

A good collection is built on known values. Dolls whose prices have been consistently high over the years should be part of a collection.

In planning or upgrading your collection, have a goal, plan or theme to make collecting more exciting. Buy the best dolls your budget will allow. Upgrade from there. Most good doll collections constantly grow and change. When a collection becomes stagnant, the owner may lose interest.

Bisque, French, A. Thuillier, 19 inches, marked *A9T*.
Stephanie is dressed in her original dress and bonnet. A.T. dolls may be the best examples of dolls with universal appeal. The longer you have them, the better you like them. They are excellent investments.

Good dolls have universal appeal. For resale, a collection should have dolls people want to own. The investment collection should have some rare or scarce dolls. They enhance the value of the entire collection.

Good dolls should be displayed. Display them in original costumes, if possible, or in copies of costumes. Copies of costumes should be made by a good seamstress.

Dolls must be kept in good condition. This means they must be kept away from insects, moisture and excessive light. Dolls should always be as clean as possible.

Don't have too many cracked or broken dolls. These may give the impression you collect imperfect dolls. Imperfections make your collection hard to sell. A museum building a collection would probably view this differently. Museums collect examples for the public to view and enjoy. A cracked, rare doll is better than no doll at all. People go to a museum to see dolls without examining each one for minute faults.

If your collection has most of the preceding qualities, it is an *investment collection*. It should increase in value.

IDENTIFYING DOLLS

Most collectors learn to identify dolls as they collect. This is one thing a beginner should learn and continually work on. Eventually it becomes easier to do. Books on dolls are necessary. Coleman's *The Collector's Encyclopedia of Dolls* is a good reference for beginners.

Many good dolls are passed up because an inexperienced buyer is unable to identify the doll and determine its value. Some valuable dolls are discarded because of the owner's lack of knowledge. Some collectors sell dolls below value because they only remember the original price they paid for the doll.

Many dolls are marked with numbers and letters on back of the head or neck. You may have to unglue the hair to find everything. Letters usually stand for the company that made the

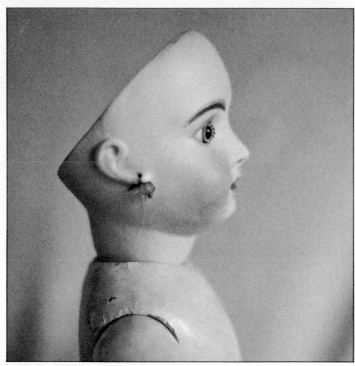

Bisque, French, H-doll, marked _H1_.
This head is typical of a French doll. The bisque of the head is cut on a slant. Ears are pierced for earrings and eyes are paperweight. The head is a swivel type on a wood and composition body. These dolls usually, but not always, have cork pates.

Bisque, French, Bru, 23-1/2 inches, marked _Bru Jne 10_.
The Smiling Bru on the right has a composition body.

doll. One number may be the mold number and another number indicates size. There may be no markings.

Take care of old clothing, no matter how dirty or disintegrated it is. Old clothing is part of the doll's value. Check the soles of shoes. Marking on the soles was a way of advertising. When the doll was sitting down, marks on the shoes could be read. These marks may give a clue to the doll's history.

Try to identify your doll by looking up its initials and numbers in a doll book. If you can't find it, send the description and a photo to someone who can. Photos of the doll should be taken with and without clothing. Include the following information in your description.

1. Letters and numbers as they appear on the doll.

2. Markings or labels. Labels in the dress or on the bottom of shoes may help establish history or value.

3. Height of the doll.

4. Material the head is made of, such as bisque.
5. Look at the mouth if the doll is bisque. Note if it is open, with teeth, or closed. This helps determine when the doll was made.
6. Check the eyes. Some are sleep eyes, which open and close. Others are paperweight eyes.
7. Material the body is made of, such as cloth, leather or composition.
8. Type of wig or painted hair.
9. Any cracks and broken or missing parts.
10. Record the condition of any clothing.

If you want an appraisal of a doll, _all_ this information is necessary.

Identification— You may want to identify a particular doll. The best place to find information is a doll shop, dealer or auction house that offers the service. You will be charged a fee if research is part of their business. Don't expect anyone to spend hours researching your dolls at no charge to you, unless they volunteer to do so. Most collectors enjoy helping you identify a doll. Be considerate and reasonable.

Gathering Information

There are many sources of information about dolls. Magazines, price guides and resource books help keep you abreast of what is happening in the doll world. Doll clubs can keep you in touch with other collectors and events that are occurring. The following information will help you learn about dolls.

MAGAZINES

You can keep up with current events in the doll world by reading Gary Ruddell's *The Doll Reader*. A bimonthly magazine, it contains articles and up-to-date information.

The Doll Reader has a color cover and 10 or more color pages. Most of the articles are about old dolls. Modern doll artists are also covered. The magazine contains advertisments for doll-making materials, doll shows, auctions and reproduction dolls for sale. This magazine also gives addresses of companies selling wigs, parts and other items for repairing old dolls.

Another magazine for doll collectors is called *Dolls*. It has a color cover and many color pages. It provides information for every level of doll collector, from beginning to advanced. It is published quarterly.

Bisque, French, Jumeau, 16 inches.
Dolls under 16 inches are called *cabinet-size dolls*. The doll at left wears contemporary clothing.

The baby doll and larger doll in the picture above are fun to collect. The baby doll wears her original gown. The larger doll wears a child's dress.

PRICE GUIDES

A doll collector should have one or two current price guides on dolls. These are only *guides*. No one can judge how much you should pay for a doll or the value of a given doll. Doll prices vary in different parts of the country. Prices vary with the size and condition of the dolls.

Jan Faulk has a series of price guides. They are called *The Blue Book Of Doll Values*. Marlene Leuzzi also has a series of doll price guides. Guides help you keep up with changes in prices.

REFERENCE BOOKS

Books can give the collector a background in doll history. It is helpful to read everything available on dolls. Check your library or bookstore for these books.

● *The Jumeau Doll Story*, by Nina S. Davies, Washington, D.C., Hobby House, 1957.
This is a translation of an original French booklet by J. Cusset, originally published in 1885. It contains photographs of Jumeau, his factory and a few dolls.

● *The Collector's Encyclopedia of Dolls*, by Dorothy, Elizabeth and Evelyn Coleman, New York, Crown Inc., 1968.
This is an important resource book for doll collectors. It lists and defines many dolls and terms useful to a collector.

● *Beautiful Dolls*, by Jon Noble, New York, Hawthorne Books Inc., 1971.
This is a book of photographs of dolls.

● *The Dolls of Yesterday*, by Eleanor St. George, New York, Scribner's, 1948.
There are several St. George books. They are old and there is more recent material available, but they contain interesting history.

● *Dolls*, by Max Boehm, New York, Dover, 1972.
This is a history of dolls.

● *The Jumeau Story*, by Margaret Whitton, New York, Dover, 1980.
This book contains color photos of Jumeaus. If you study it, you will know what to look for in a Jumeau.

● *The Collector's History of Dolls*, by C.E. King, New York, St. Martins, 1977.
This book provides excellent background material on old dolls.

DOLL CLUBS

Many doll collectors are not affiliated with a doll club. However, if you like people and club activities, a doll-club membership may be for you.

Bisque, French, A. Thuillier, 12 inches, marked *A.T. 2*. Blue paperweight eyes, a leather body and bisque hands make this doll attractive.

This picture shows the fine handmade lace and linen underclothing of the doll.

The United Federation of Doll Clubs (UFDC) is the largest doll club, with approximately 16,000 members. It is divided into 16 regions across the country. Each region has a director and many clubs located in and around most cities. The UFDC has a national convention each year. Regions also have conventions. These conventions are open to club members only.

To become a member of the UFDC, you must own some old dolls, then locate a club that is not full. There are members-at-large who live in areas where there are no clubs.

The UFDC publishes a magazine four times a year, which is available only to members. If you are interested in joining the UFDC, write 8 East St., Parksville, MO 64152.

The next-largest doll club is the Doll Artisan Guild (DAG). It has approximately 5,000 members, many outside the United States. I founded this group in 1977 as an organization for porcelain-reproduction-doll makers. Since doll makers usually collect dolls, and doll collectors often make dolls, the DAG has many members. Membership is not restricted.

The DAG magazine is published six times a year. The Guild runs the Doll City Doll Show each year in Oneonta, New York, for the benefit of the American Cancer Society. Every other year, there is an international convention, also held in Oneonta. For information, write The Doll Artisan Guild, 35 Main St., Oneonta, NY 13820.

There are two clubs for makers of original dolls. They are the Original Doll Artists Council of America (ODACA) and the National Institute of American Doll Artists (NIADA). Smaller specialty clubs also exist, such as the Kewpie Collector Club, Ginnie Doll Club, Grace Dayton Club and others.

You may be interested in starting a doll club. It can be done with a notice in the newspaper or on a public bulletin board, or by word of mouth. A few hard workers can start a club. Doll club meetings are usually held in members' homes. The number of club members is usually limited to the size of the meeting places.

Corresponding with other doll collectors may serve the same purposes as a club. For many people, correspondence is a convenient way to keep up with what's happening in the doll world. For collectors who live in isolated areas, are handicapped or cannot travel easily, it's a way to remain aware of doll events.

Glossary

The following terms will help you understand dolls. Read the definitions and study the pictures. These terms are used throughout the book.

A.M.—Bisque dolls made by Armand Marseille, a German doll maker, from about 1895 to 1925.

A.T.—Dolls probably made by A. Thuillier. They had leather bodies, as well as jointed, composition bodies.

Absentee bid—Bidding at auction, either by mail or phone, without being there in person.

An *A.T.* doll, probably made by Thuillier.

Adams, Emma—Emma Adams made rag dolls. She painted the features and hair on every doll she made until her death in 1900.

Advertising dolls—Doll made to advertise or promote a product, such as Campbell's Soup kids or the Morton's Salt Girl.

All-bisque—Term used when the entire doll is made of bisque.

Antique—Dolls over 75 years old.

Applied ears—Ears made separately from the head and attached after the head is removed from mold. Found in older French dolls.

Articulation—When used with dolls, refers to the jointing for possible movement.

Baby Bo Kaye—A boy baby doll with celluloid or bisque head, composition limbs, cloth body, voice box and molded hair. Copyrighted in 1926.

Bald heads—Dome-shape heads without hair.

Ball-jointed—A type of doll joint using a wood ball in the socket for flexibility in movement.

Bébé—French childlike doll.

Beecher dolls—Mrs. Thomas K. Beecher made knit fabric dolls.

This is a *ball-jointed* F.G. doll below. Note the ball joints in her knees, hips and arms.

Belton-type—Bisque head made with two or more holes in the top, possibly to fasten a wig. Head is sometimes flattened, but not cut open.
Bent-limb—Baby-type body in sitting position.
Bergoin—Name found on Steiner dolls.

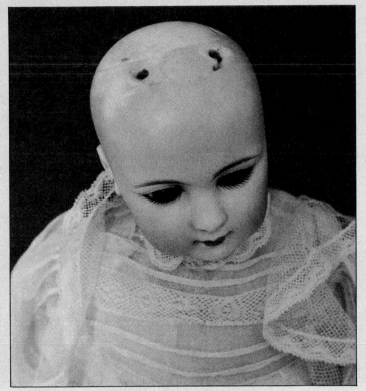

A *Belton-type*. The doll shows the bald head with holes, possibly to fasten a wig. This one, made by Simon and Halbig, is numbered 919. Not all Belton-type dolls are French—this one is German.

Biedermeier—China dolls with a black spot painted on top of head and no hair.
Biskoline—Type of dull celluloid.
Bisque—A form of porcelain clay, fired or baked until it has chemically changed or melted. It is like the material of a fine dish, only without a glaze or shine. See china head.
Blown eyes—Sphere-shape glass eyes that have been blown in their creation.
Blush—Rosy color applied to cheeks, backs of hands and other parts of a doll's body.
Bonnie Babe—Name of baby dolls made by Georgene Averill.
Breveté—French word for *patented*.
Brownies—Cloth dolls based on the figures of Palmer Cox. Twelve different dolls appeared on one yard of cloth. Each doll had a front and back to cut out, which were sewn together and stuffed.

Bru—A French doll-making company.
  Jne—Junior, found on Brus.
  Nursing Bru—Bru doll with an open mouth and a nursing mechanism.
Bye-Lo Baby—Baby doll designed and copyrighted by Grace Storey Putnam. The doll was fashioned after a 3-day-old baby and was first made in wax. The body was made of cloth and stuffed.
Cabinet-size doll—A doll under 16 inches high.

This is a *candy-store doll* named *Chubby*. He is a small figure with jointed arms.

Candy-store dolls—Small, inexpensive, all-bisque dolls, originally sold in candy stores.
Carriage trade—Wealthy people who purchased expensive dolls, such as Jumeau and Bru, for their children.
Celluloid—Originally, this was the trade name for dolls made by the Hyatt Brothers. Dolls were made of a synthetic material composed of cellulose nitrate, camphor, pigments, fillers and alcohol.

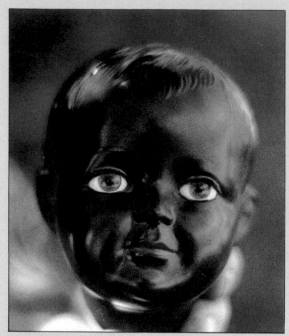

Celluloid, marked *France*. This doll has inset glass eyes.

A *china head*. Note the high gloss.

Character dolls—Lifelike representations of real people, especially children and babies. Dolls with realistic expressions.

Chase, Martha—Martha Chase made dolls with heads of stockinette fabric, stretched over a mask, which had raised features. Features were hand-painted. Bodies were cloth and stuffed with cotton. An area was left unstuffed at each joint so arms and legs could move.

China head—Glazed porcelain shoulder heads with a shiny surface. Unglazed ceramic is *bisque* and glazed ceramic is *china*.

Collectable—Dolls which are 25 to 75 years old.

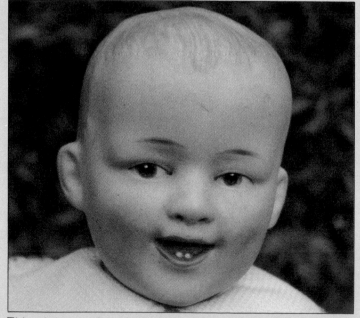

This *character doll* by Heubach looks like a real boy.

Collectable dolls are between 25 and 75 years old. This is a Madame Alexander doll, which is a collectable. She has crude composition and painted facial features.

These *color rubs* appear on the doll's cheek. Color rubs usually indicate the doll was played with.

Color rubs—Places where cheek color is rubbed off.

Composition—A mixture of paper pulp, wood pulp and glue. It was used to make entire doll or jointed bodies.

Contemporary clothes—Clothing made about the time of the doll, but not necessarily the doll's original clothing.

Crèche figures—Figures used in religious scenes. These are sometimes collected as dolls.

Crown—Open-crown or closed-crown refers to the bisque over the top of the head. This was usually cut off to set in glass eyes. *Belton-type* is the term used for closed crowns.

D.R.G.M.—Registered design: *Deutsches Reichs Gegraughs Muster*.

Dolly Dingle—Doll designed by Grace Drayton.

F.G.—Initials found on some dolls made by Françoise Gauthier, a French doll maker.

Flange necks—Type of neck usually found on baby dolls. A roll or flange on the neck widens to hold head in a cloth body.

Flirty eyes—Eyes that move from side to side.

French fashion dolls—French lady dolls of the late 19th century, dressed in beautiful costumes.

Frozen Charlotte—An unjointed doll of bisque or china. A few had molded hair, bonnets or wigs.

Fulper—An American company, Fulper Pottery made bisque heads and some all-bisque dolls. A few heads had molded hair and painted eyes.

Gauthier, Françoise—A French doll-head maker.

Gesland body—A stuffed body with a wire frame and stockinette covering. Made by Gesland.

Gladdie—Doll designed by Trobridge.

Glaze—Smooth and glossy glasslike finish on porcelain.

Googly eyes—Eyes with pupil set or painted to the side.

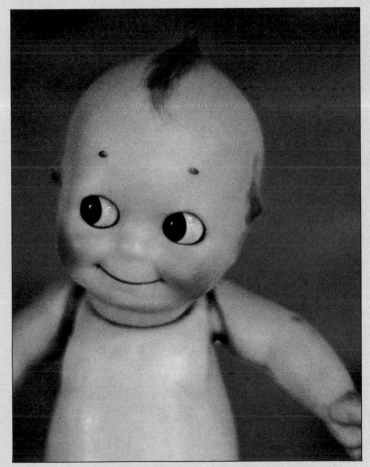

Googly eyes. Kewpies and other bisque dolls have large, side-set eyes.

The *flirty eyes* close on this doll, as well as move from side to side. She is a K(star)R 117N doll.

Greiner-type—Composition doll made in the United States.

Gusset—Piece of leather or cloth inserted in joint of a cloth or leather body to make the joint movable.

These three dolls are *hand-sculptured*. They all started as lumps of clay and were made to represent the children in Longfellow's poem, *The Children's Hour.*

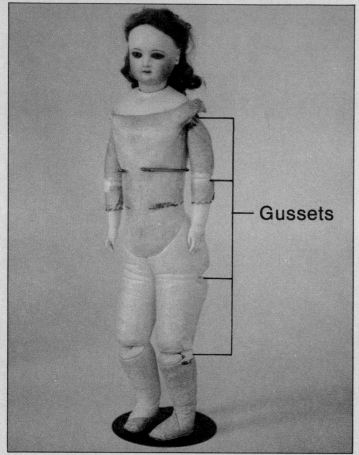

Gussets

This undressed lady doll shows where *gussets* are placed to make joints.

Gutsell—A cloth boy doll.

Hairline crack—A small crack.

Hand-sculptured—Modeled by hand from a lump of clay.

Heubach—German maker of character dolls.

High cheek color—Lots of pink blush was added to the cheeks.

Huret—A French doll maker.

Incised—Indented or cut into doll.

Intaglio eyes—Painted eyes with pupil incised or indented.

Jumeau—A French doll-making company.

   Déposé—Registered.

   E.J.—Emile Jumeau.

   Incised Déposé—The word déposé is indented.

   Long Face—Modeling of the face is long on early Jumeaus.

   Stamped—Markings are stamped, instead of incised.

A *Heubach doll,* which is a character doll.

A small character doll made by *Kestner*.

The *Action Kewpie* on the left represents a farmer.

The *lady doll* on the right is by Kestner. She has a fully developed figure.

K(star)R—The doll-making company of Kammer and Reinhardt. A star symbol is between the K and the R on the label.

Kestner—A doll-making company.

Kewpie—Dolls designed by Rose O'Neill that had a unique appearance. The doll represented a fat child without clothes, with molded short hair. Kewpies were made of various materials, in many sizes. Some represented various occupations.

Kidiline—Inexpensive substitute for leather in doll bodies.

Lady dolls—Dolls with an adult-female figure.

Laughing Baby—One of Georgene Averill's baby dolls.

Mason-Taylor—Makers of Springfield wooden dolls.

Markings—The doll's identification letters or symbols usually incised or stamped on the back of the doll's neck or head.

Marque, Albert—A sculptor who made dolls with bisque heads and composition bodies. The faces of Marque dolls are alike, because he used only one mold.

Marseille, Armand—A German doll maker.

Mechanicals—Dolls that perform in some way. Actions are activated by an enclosed mechanism. Many feature music boxes.

Milliner's Models—Dolls with papier-mâché heads and wooden limbs that don't move.

Miniatures (Minis)—Dolls under 5 inches high.

A *mechanical doll*. She is supposed to be waiting for a friend who didn't show up. She stamps her foot and moves her handkerchief to her eyes as her music box plays.

Mint—Original condition, not restored.
Molded clothing—Clothing formed in the mold of the doll, not made of cloth.
Molded-hair toddlers—Dolls with the hair formed in the mold. Real hair was not added.
Motschmann-type—Doll made with fabric or leather inserts for movement. This technique was copied from the Japanese.
Multifaced dolls—Head turns, exposing different expressions.
Name dolls—Dolls that have names incised on them by the manufacturer, rather than names given by the owners.
Nodders—All-bisque dolls whose heads are loose, but held on with elastic or other means, so they move easily.
Open-closed mouth—Mouth modeled in open position, but with no opening through the bisque.

A *Milliner's Model* is shown at left. It is an old papier-mâché doll with wooden arms and legs, and a leather torso.

The little doll on the right displays many things. He is a *miniature*, under 5 inches high. He has *molded clothing*, which means the clothing was part of the mold. He is a *nodder*—his head moves because it is fastened only with elastic.

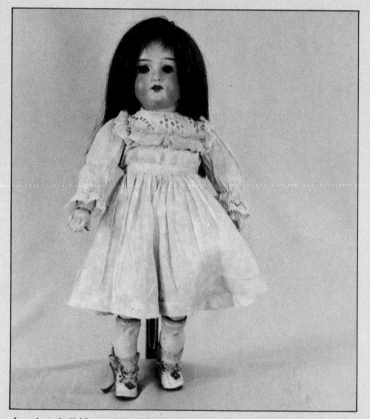

A *mint doll*. Her original body is in excellent condition. She is wearing her original wig, clothing and shoes, all in top condition.

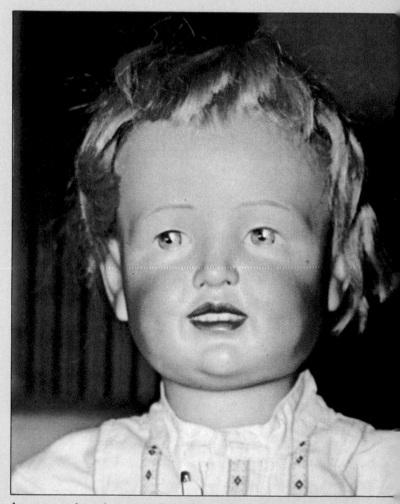

An *open-closed mouth*. This Simon and Halbig boy doll shows his teeth (open), but there is no opening in the bisque (closed).

This wax doll is one of a kind and is considered an *original doll.*

These are also *original dolls.* They were made in England. The heads are nuts and the bodies are cloth. According to family records, they were made around 1880.

Original doll—This term is often misused. It usually refers to an original doll made of unfired clay. A mold is made of the doll, and in the process, the original doll is destroyed. But true original dolls are those of carved wood, needlework and some rag dolls. It is a one-of-a-kind doll.

Paperweight eyes—Eyes with a glass bulge on the outside, giving depth to the eye. Used mostly on French dolls.

Parian—When used with dolls, it means a white porcelain. Collectors sometimes refer to untinted bisque dolls as *parian.*

Parisiènne—French lady dolls.

Pate—The covering for the open head (crown). This is usually cardboard in German dolls and cork in French dolls.

Peddlers—Dolls representing street sellers carrying their wares.

Penny woodens—Small, jointed, all-wood dolls with no fine details. They sold for pennies.

Plaster pates—A pate made of plaster instead of cardboard or cork.

Porcelain—High-fired, translucent, vitrified clays. May be unglazed, called *bisque,* glazed, called *china,* or white, unglazed with no over-tinting, called *parian.*

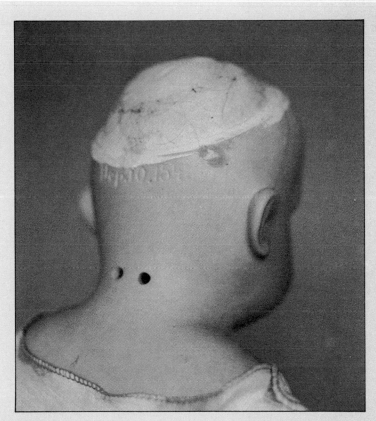

A *plaster pate.* Kestner used plaster pates for the heads of his dolls. French doll makers used cork pates.

Portrait doll—Head modeled to resemble a person, often a celebrity.

Printed dolls—Doll and clothing printed on yard goods to be cut and sewn, then stuffed by purchaser. Also called *cloth doll, rag doll* or *art-fabric-type doll.*

Queen Anne—Type of wooden doll.

Reproduction dolls—Dolls made by making a mold from an existing doll. Reproductions are always at least 16% smaller than the original doll.

Reproduction head—A head made from a mold of an existing doll.

SFBJ—This stands for the *Société Française de Fabrication des Bébés and Jouets.* The SFBJ was a group of doll makers that made dolls after 1898. They collaborated to make dolls to sell at lower prices. They produced the most common examples of French dolls.

S.G.D.G.—Without government guarantee, used with Breveté.

S.H.900s—A series of Simon and Halbig dolls with bald heads.

Schmitt—A French doll-making company.

Head of this *reproduction doll* is made from a mold of Kestner's Gibson Girl.

This is a *portrait doll* of Rose O'Neill, sculptured by Leta Wilson and painted by Muriel Kramer.

Simon and Halbig *900 series.* This doll's number is 929.

Schoenhut—A doll-making firm that made wooden dolls in Philadelphia from 1912 to the 1930s.

Shoulder head—Doll's head and shoulders are in one piece.

Shoulder plate—The top shoulder part of a doll, having an indentation for the neck to fit into.

Simon and Halbig—A doll-making firm.

Skippy—A composition doll designed to look like the cartoon character, Skippy, created by Percy L. Crosby.

Sleep eyes—Eyes with a closing mechanism.

Split head—Wax heads that were slit open to insert hair, then closed.

Springfield dolls—Jointed wooden dolls made in Vermont by Joel Ellis and Mason-Taylor.

Stamped doll—Doll with markings stamped on its neck or body.

Steiner—A doll-making firm.

    Kicking Steiner—A mechanized Steiner that kicks.

    Walking Steiner—A mechanized Steiner that walks.

Stringing—Putting a jointed composition body together with elastic.

Swivel head—One-piece head and neck that turns in socket of shoulder plate.

Thuillier—A. Thuillier was a French doll maker.

Tête mark—A Jumeau mark. *Tête Jumeau.*

Tuck comb—A small carved comb in the top of the hair. Used on some wooden, jointed dolls.

Tynie Baby—A baby doll with a bisque or composition head, soft body and voice box.

Unbroken wrists—Stiff wrists. Gauntlet-type wrists are unjointed composition. The hand and lower arm are in one piece.

Vendor doll—Same as peddler doll.

Wax-over—To recoat with wax.

Wire-eye—Sleep-eye dolls made with a lever at the side of head to close the eyes.

Worn body—A doll that was played with until the paint was partly worn off.

Yeux fibres—Eyes with white rays radiating from the pupil.

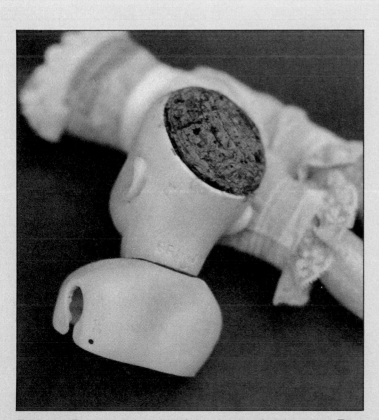

This is a Bru *shoulder plate.* It is open under the arms. The head swivels on this shoulder plate. Note the cork pate.

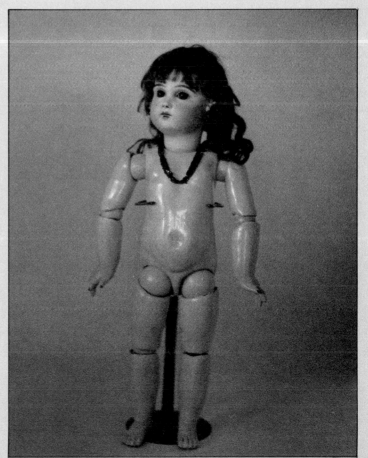

Unbroken wrists are usually found on a French doll body like this one. There is no joint at the wrist.

Collecting for Less than $200

People often want to know how much money they need to start a doll collection. They ask if good dolls at "reasonable" prices are still available. The answer is "yes"—there are still good dolls available for less than $200.

Many people start collecting by unpacking childhood dolls, rummaging through the attic or gathering dolls from relatives. Others begin by purchasing unwanted dolls from friends or neighbors. Most women had dolls as children. Many still have them today, packed away somewhere.

The first time a collector's doll is purchased is a disaster for many people. That was the case with us. There were no books telling what to look for or how to purchase a doll. Today, there are many resource books available to help you select the right doll for you. This book gives you guidelines to help you buy the best doll for your money.

Bisque, German, marked *Armand Marseille 390, Germany.* This doll has an open mouth, four teeth, brown human hair and a jointed, composition body. As she walks, her head turns. She was given to me when I was 6 years old. She was purchased at Macy's and came without clothes. She had some material with her and my mother made her clothing. The clothing was lost, so I re-dressed her and gave her to my daughter, Colleen, when she was 6. This doll still wears a dress made to match Colleen's.

Clowns are fun to collect. The one shown above cost under $200.

Wood, Swiss.
The carved shoulder head and jointed, carved arms of this wooden doll make it one of a kind.

START WITH LESS-EXPENSIVE DOLLS

You can start your collection with less-expensive dolls. Later, you may be able to buy dolls of higher value. Or you can save your money until you have enough to buy one good doll.

There are many good dolls that can be purchased for under $200 that may increase in value in the future.

You must hunt for dolls to collect. Usually the best, least-expensive dolls are purchased directly from original owners. This eliminates the auctioneer's expense or the dealer's markup. Put an advertisement in a local paper telling people you wish to buy dolls. It may help you locate what you're looking for.

Yard, garage and tag sales are good places to begin. Flea markets or swap meets might also produce something. Put notices on bulletin boards at laundries, grocery stores and other public places.

Sometimes fine dolls can be purchased for a small sum. The owner may be tired of having them in a drawer or moving them from place to place. Or the family may not be interested in the dolls and the owner may be looking for a good home for them. Some people prefer to give their dolls away rather than sell them. Dolls that are in pieces or unstrung can often be purchased for a lower price.

With effort, you may find dolls to buy for under $200. The actual value of the dolls may be much more.

Rag doll.
A 16-inch Kathy Kruse doll as she appeared at auction. Considered a rag doll, this doll has been produced since 1910.

SOME GOOD INVESTMENTS

Dolls with actual values of less than $200 can be good investments. There are many dolls in this category. They can be collected for fun or investment.

First, plan what you want to purchase, then buy carefully. You must proceed with a well-outlined plan so your collection will have value and appeal. If you choose carefully, your dolls can grow into a small investment. Some dolls, such as advertising dolls or Kewpies, are worth more in a collection than they are individually.

Below is a list of dolls that may cost less than $200 to purchase.

Schoenhuts
Kewpies
Small all-bisque dolls
Alexanders
Painted bisque dolls
Storybook dolls
Small Armand Marseille dolls
Some baby dolls
Some Milliner's Models
SFBJs in costumes
Undressed dolls
Cloth dolls
Advertising dolls
Craft dolls from different countries,
 showing costumes
Reproduction dolls

When buying bisque dolls for a low price, be careful. A doll may have replaced parts, a hidden crack or a reproduction body. Check each doll carefully. Look for legs or arms that don't match, broken teeth, permanently set sleep eyes and other imperfections.

Composition, American, Effanbee, 1929.
Skippy has a five-piece body, painted hair and eyes, and original clothing. Skippy was a comic strip character created by Percy L. Crosby. Note the cracking in composition.

Papier-mâché, German.
The papier-mâché construction of the 1920s is shown in this doll. Her fine condition is unusual. She has a swivel head, painted eyes and a five-piece body construction. Her dress is organdy and she wears a matching one-piece cotton undersuit. Her hair is flapper-style. She is in mint condition.

Cloth, American, 14-1/2 inches.
Little Lulu was made about 1958. She has a cloth face, painted features and string hair. Little Lulu is from the comic strip by Marjorie Buell. Her clothing is original. This is a late example of a cloth doll.

Composition.
This Oriental doll has a swivel head and a five-piece baby body. Her original clothing is deteriorating.

Composition, American.
Dolly Dingle was designed by Grace Drayton about 1910. The composition is still in good condition. She wears her original outfit.

Cloth, printed, Brownie, 7-1/2 inches.
This doll, which represents Uncle Sam, is by Palmer Cox. It was copyrighted in 1892. The copyright mark is on the foot.

Little Red Riding Hood material.
Dolls were printed on yard goods. They were sold and sewn together at home. Each took about a yard of material. Arnold Print Works made this doll and many others. This Little Red Riding Hood is dated 1892.

At left is an original Marque doll (the larger one) and a reproduction Marque doll (the smaller one). The reproduction Marque was the most expensive, limited-edition reproduction doll made. The price was high because the original doll and the mold cost a great deal.

The doll at top right is a reproduction of a Stobé doll. The dress is also a reproduction. Reproductions should be marked with the reproduction artist's signature or mark, plus old markings. A reproduction doll should be an *exact duplicate* of the original.

REPRODUCTION DOLLS

One of the most beautiful and fun-to-collect types of dolls priced under $200 are reproductions of famous old dolls. These reproductions should be signed by the reproduction artist.

For top value, they should have composition bodies like originals. The new composition is a hard, dull, rubberlike material. It looks like the old composition. Reproductions put on bisque bodies are heavy. They chip, break and are incorrect. A reproduction is an *exact* copy of the old doll, except a reproduction is always at least 16% smaller than the original.

This is a close-up of Stobé reproduction.

Bisque, Reproduction Long-Face Jumeau.
Connie Walser Derek made this reproduction Long-Face Jumeau.

Study reproduction dolls carefully before you buy one. Know exactly what you are looking for and what you want. It is best to check your reference books. Know the materials, construction and features of the original doll before you buy any reproduction doll. A reproduction should look as much like the original doll as possible.

You might want to collect reproductions of old French and German dolls. Some modern doll artists rival old master doll makers. These copies of antiques are accurate and beautiful.

When signed by the reproduction artist, these dolls are valuable, fun to collect and provide enjoyment for a collector. Many can be purchased for less than $200. In the future, these beautiful dolls may be heirlooms.

A reproduction doll could have been purchased in the 1970s for less than $100. In 1981, a reproduction doll called the *Albert Mark* doll was made in a limited edition. It sold for $850. Most reproduction dolls cost between $125 and $375.

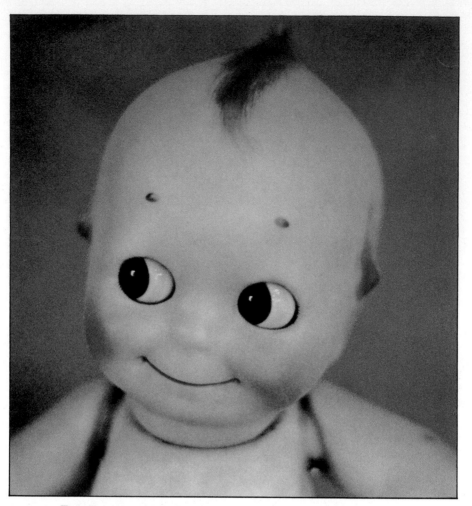

This Kewpie doll has molded short hair. Kewpies are popular with collectors because dolls are made of many different materials, in many sizes.

KEWPIE DOLLS

Kewpies are fun and popular to collect. A Kewpie doll represents a fat child without clothing, with molded short hair. Made of various materials, these dolls come in many sizes.

Some people collect stories, books, poetry and illustrations by Rose O'Neill, the woman who created Kewpies. If you plan to collect Kewpies, locate a club that specializes in them. It will be fun and educational to belong to it. Kewpies were first produced in 1913.

Action Kewpies are more sought-after than plain Kewpies. Action Kewpies have an accessory, such as a gun, umbrella, hat or book.

Some Kewpies are marked with a paper label with the words *Design Patent* in a circle. On the bottom, there is a copyright symbol.

In the 1950s, the Cameo Company used original molds and reissued some Kewpies. The bisque on these was rough and more highly tinted. The reissue doll has gray eyelashes instead of black. It has painted, flat highlights in the eyes instead of molded relief. The Rose O'Neill signature is on the feet. These were the last authentic Kewpies made.

WHERE TO START

A small household auction that includes dolls is a good place to find dolls to start your collection. A doll auction to sell one person's collection could include dolls of all values.

Theriault's Auctions, which travels from one large city to another, has uncataloged auctions following the regular cataloged one. Uncataloged auctions are filled with lower-priced dolls. Sometimes there are bargains to be found. A buyer must be alert and knowledgable because dolls cannot be returned. There is no absentee bidding at these auctions.

Withington Auctions, of Concord, New Hampshire, sells dolls of various prices. If you travel to an auction, include the cost of travel and other expenses in the value of the doll to you.

Doll magazines may advertise some dolls for under $200. Follow the guidelines on page 127 for ordering by mail.

Many people buy dolls and pay for them over a period of time. Some dealers sell dolls this way. This method can be a way of saving. Paying for dolls this way costs more because of interest charges. Be careful before you finance the purchase of a doll. Choose dolls wisely.

Bisque, French, Jumeau, marked 9.
All Long-Face Jumeaus have applied ears. This doll has unusual deep gray-green eyes, a brown human-hair wig and an original silk-taffeta dress. The Long-Face Jumeau, also called a *Cody Jumeau,* is a top collector's choice. Be sure unmarked heads are on Jumeau-marked bodies or Simonne bodies. Few dolls are found in original clothing. You must decide from the modeling whether or not it is a Long-Face Jumeau. It is sometimes difficult for the beginner without another doll for comparison.

Theriault's Auctions are held in or near large cities. The auction moves from city to city, and occurs about once a month.

Collecting Bisque Dolls

People collect dolls for different reasons. Some collect dolls by makers, size or because they belong to a particular group. Many dolls are collected according to the material from which the doll is made. People collect bisque dolls, which have bisque heads only. Other collectors prefer composition dolls or cloth dolls. Any doll made of a particular material is collectable to them. A doll is categorized by the material its *head* is made of. If it is made entirely of one material, the word *all* is added, such as *all-bisque* doll.

Many bisque-doll collectors narrow their collection to French bisque, German bisque or American bisque. These categories can be subdivided again into other collections.

BISQUE DOLLS

Bisque dolls have beauty and lasting characteristics that make them a good investment. Old bisque doll heads don't deteriorate or discolor with age. Moths don't eat holes in them, like they do with felt or cloth. Heads don't melt or mar, as wax heads do. The bisque appears flesh-like. Painting and tinting are fired in and become part of the porcelain. Features cannot peel or flake off, as does paint on wood or composition dolls. The face of a hundred-year-old bisque doll is as pretty and colorful as the day it was made.

Bisque dolls have the highest values and are the best investment possibilities. Their lasting beauty also makes them enjoyable to own.

Bisque, French, Gauthier, marked *FG.*
The beautiful doll shown at left adds value to a collection.

Kestner's *Hilda Baby* is shown at top. It is a collector's prize.

Bisque, French, 20 inches, marked with crescent.
The old dress and ornate hat may be original on this doll. She has paperweight eyes. This doll, and similar dolls, are sometimes sold as Marque dolls. It is *not* a Marque doll. There is a very slight resemblance, but the bisque is poor, as are details and painting. If this photo were in an auction catalog, you might spend more money than you should, as we did.

Bisque, French, 18 inches, marked *Eden Bébé 1*.
The cobalt-blue eyes of this doll make it different. Her brunette wig is human hair. She is wearing a reproduction dress. The painting on this doll is a little crude, but she adds value to a collection.

DIFFERENCES IN BISQUE DOLLS

As you collect bisque dolls, you will become knowledgable about the similarities in dolls. An accomplished collector can determine by the sculpture and painting which dolls are made by a specific company. Doll "families" have similarities to each other. Members of these families share a common resemblance.

An accomplished doll collector can look at a row of dolls and name their makers according to family resemblance. But dolls from the same factory can also show a difference in standard of workmanship in bisque, painting and costumes. This difference makes collecting more exciting.

BEST BISQUE DOLLS

Some bisque dolls are valuable to collect. The quality of workmanship and their rarity is reflected in the prices they bring. The most valuable dolls today were made by Albert Marque, A. Thuillier, Huret, Bru, Jumeau, Steiner, Schmitt and F. Gauthier. The most valuable bisque dolls are discussed in detail beginning on page 98.

Bisque, French, 18 inches, marked *Eden Bébé 1*.
This is a good example of a reproduction costume. The
dress and bonnet are copied from the antique costume. This
is almost as good as an original.

Bisque, French, Fashion doll, 17 inches.
She has a swivel head, gray paperweight eyes and a fashion
body. The original costume on this doll included pantaloons,
numerous petticoats (one with a long train), a lace top, a
skirt of lace over pleated tiers, and a lace train with garlands
of pink and blue roses.

FRENCH BISQUE DOLLS

French bisque dolls are excellent investments
and pleasurable to own. Some less-valuable
dolls made by French doll makers are also good
to collect.

French fashion dolls were made with lovely
bisque heads. These dolls were French lady
dolls of the late 19th century. They were dressed
in fashionable costumes and had adult-female
figures. If a French fashion doll is stripped of old
clothing, her value decreases. A French fashion
doll with an original costume and original wig
could be a good investment, depending on her
condition.

Some French fashion dolls had wooden
bodies and special joints. Most had leather
bodies, feet and hands. The dolls with wooden
bodies are the most expensive to buy and are
best for reselling. Portrait types and unusual
sizes, such as very small or very large, are also

good investments for any doll collector.

Collections of French baby dolls will be small.
There are not many designs to choose from, but
they are good investments. A collection might
include Nursing Brus and some SFBJ babies.

SFBJ stands for the *Societé Française de Fabrication des Bébés and Jouets*. Is was a group of
doll makers that made dolls after 1898. Their
products are the most common examples of
French dolls.

SFBJ was made up of the *best* French doll
makers. They banded together to make dolls to
sell at lower prices. The group included Jumeau
and Bru doll-making firms.

SFBJ wanted to make and sell dolls to compete
with German doll prices. They had to meet
competition or go out of business. Some dolls
continued to be manufactured as usual, but after
a time these doll makers lowered standards.

Bisque, French, 18 inches.
We named this doll *Mlle. Fern.* She has pale-blue paper-weight eyes and bisque lower arms and hands. She is a beautiful lady doll. Her body, even the wooden legs and feet, are covered with twill. She is jointed to allow her to sit or pose in any position. Even her ankles are jointed.

Bisque, French, 24-1/2 inches.
This unmarked portrait lady doll has blue eyes, bisque arms and hands, applied ears and a light-auburn wig. The eyes on this old doll are not evenly cut. The bisque is fine and translucent.

By 1922, the SFBJ syndicate was producing seven million dolls a year. Today, these dolls are the most commonly found French dolls. They are usually poor quality, poor craftsmanship and poorly decorated. But if you are careful and selective, you can find some good SFBJ dolls for under $200.

Many SFBJ dolls can be recognized by their straight-down lower eyelashes. Sometimes these dolls have an orange-red face color. Many were well-dressed. Study the dolls to detect those of poor quality.

Bisque, French, Jumeau, 22-1/2 inches.
This portrait lady doll has blue eyes, a leather body, and leather hands and feet. Old portrait-type dolls are excellent investments. The bisque is pressed into the mold instead of poured. The nose and mouth indentations on the inside of the head are filled. Ears are made in a separate mold and applied to the porcelain before firing.

Bisque, French, 15-1/2 inches, marked *Aux Reves de L'enfants, Jouets, de Poupees, Articulees, Jeaux de Societe Cartonnages Instruct, Paris.*
A lady doll with light-gray paperweight eyes, this doll has a swivel head on leather body and bisque hands. The body is stamped with the name of the shop that assembled or sold it.

Bisque, French, Fashion doll, 13 inches.
The little French fashion doll at top right has an all-leather body. Her maker is unknown. She is a choice doll because of her small size and elaborate original clothing.

Bisque, French, Fashion dolls.
The two dolls at right are French fashion dolls. Their bodies are warped. They are similar in construction, but one body is in better condition. The stamp on the front of the small one could be the doll shop where it was sold, rather than the doll maker.

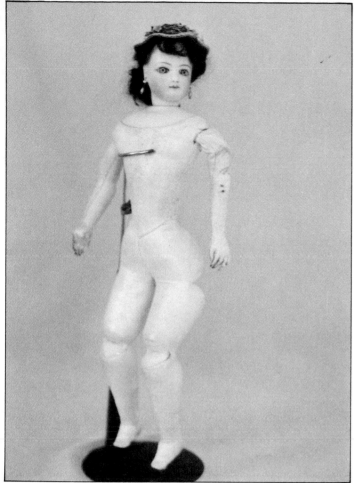

Bisque, French, 15-1/2 inches.
This unmarked lady doll has light-green eyes and a swivel head. Both pictures are the same doll, dressed and undressed. The picture on the left shows the body, which is in fine condition. Over a period of time, the sawdust in these bodies shakes down and absorbs moisture. The body expands, bending hips and legs out of shape.

Bisque, French.
Small, choice lady dolls can sometimes be purchased at reasonable prices. The one on the left wears her original costume.

Bisque, French, Bru, 15-1/2 inches, marked *Bru Jne 4*.
This doll is called a *Nursing Bru.* She has a leather body and wooden arms and legs. Her mouth is open and she has a nursing mechanism in her head.

Bisque, French, SFBJ, 15 inches, marked *SFBJ*.
The doll at top right has brown eyes, an open mouth with teeth and an original costume. It is not the best example of a collector's doll because of its poor workmanship.

Bisque, French, 10 inches, marked *Unis France 60, 71, 149*.
The body of the doll at right has a paper label. Her legs and arms are one-piece construction. Her peach-color, lace-trimmed dress, underclothing, peach shoes and hat are original. Late dolls like this make a nice addition to an under-12-inches collection. This is an example of a good doll under $200.

Bisque, French, SFBJ, 24 inches, marked *SFBJ, 252, Paris.*
Libby has blue sleep eyes with real lashes, a composition body, blond mohair wig and an old, white embroidered child's dress. She is a good example of an SFBJ. This one is expensive.

This is a close-up of the same doll. She has good proportions. Her face has excellent modeling and good painting. Note the straight-down bottom lashes.

Bisque, German, Lady Dolls.
1. R. Coburg, 18 inches. This doll is wearing original clothing. She has a leather body and hands. An unusual doll, she adds value to a collection. 2. This doll has a leather body and arms, and is wearing original clothes. 3. Simon & Halbig 1159, 18 inches. She has an open mouth with teeth. 4. A 14-inch Gibson Girl.

GERMAN BISQUE DOLLS

German bisque dolls are the most popular and easy to find of the bisque types. They are fun to have and enjoyable to look at and their values have not decreased. They usually require a smaller investment to begin collecting them and increase more slowly in value. American children played with these dolls. They are not usually found in original clothing. When they are, expect to pay more for them.

Collectors have seen the prices rise for German bisque lady dolls. In July 1981, a German World War I nurse doll sold for over $9,000 at auction.

Bisque, German, unmarked.
The German lady doll's modeling and blue eyes are charming.

Bisque, German, Simon and Halbig, 22 inches.
The doll at top right is wearing a copy of her antique dress.

Bisque, German, Kestner, 12 inches.
A small but delightful doll to collect, the doll on the right is in mint condition. She has her original clothing and wig.

Dolls by the Kestner doll-making company are good examples of German collector's dolls. Their prices increase consistently but not rapidly. When buying German dolls, look for smooth bisque, sleep eyes that open and close, and an old wig and costume.

German bisque baby dolls are exciting investments. For a few years, the price of regular baby dolls increased little. In 1980, the price of an ordinary baby doll began to rise. This may be because German doll collectors began buying among themselves.

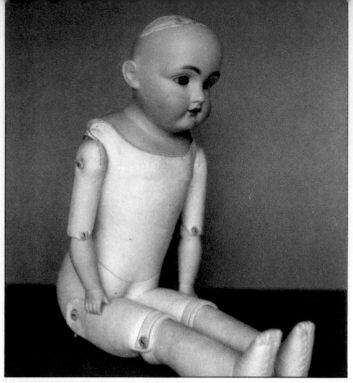

Bisque, German, Kestner, 16 inches.
This doll has a leather body. She is pin-jointed and has a shoulder head. Kestner dolls often have plaster pates, as this one shows. German collector's doll prices do not increase rapidly, but climb consistently. When buying German dolls, look for smooth bisque, sleep eyes that work, and old wig and costume.

Bisque, German, Schoenau and Hoffmeister, 40 inches, marked *P.B.* in a star and *S.H.*
Extra-large dolls have increased in price from $100 to $1,000 recently. This doll has an open mouth with four teeth and a composition body. These dolls were the ones most older people played with as children. They are dear to many collectors. Do not confuse these dolls with those made by Simon and Halbig.

Bisque, German, 28 inches, marked *1914*, © J.D.K. Jr., Gesgesch 1070.
The molded, brush-stroked hair of *Hilda* is part of her value. She has a bent-limb, composition body and brown sleep eyes. This is the largest size made. A Hilda baby doll with this type of head is a good investment. This same doll was also made with an open head, to take a wig. The closed-head doll is more valuable than the doll with a wig. This doll is owned by Betty Allison.

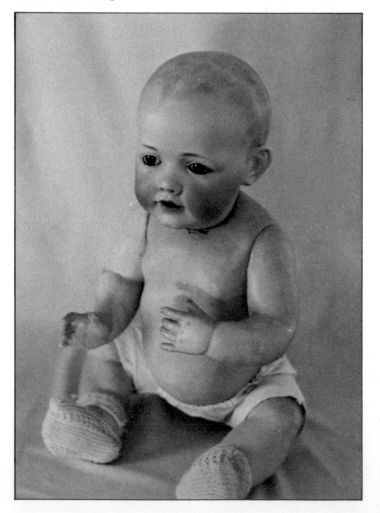

Some small baby dolls can be purchased for $200 or less. Other fine, large baby dolls cost more than $2,000. An example is a Hilda doll. It has steadily increased in price since 1973. Baby dolls present a problem for most collectors. They take up a lot of space because they can only sit.

The most expensive group of German bisque dolls to collect are the Heubachs and the K(star)R character dolls. The K(star)R doll is actually marked K, with a 6-point star, followed by an R. For our references, we will use K(star)R. Character dolls were lifelike representations of real people, especially children and babies. These dolls had realistic expressions. They rival or surpass some French dolls in value. Closed-mouth German bisque children dolls are charming. The lips on these dolls are closed.

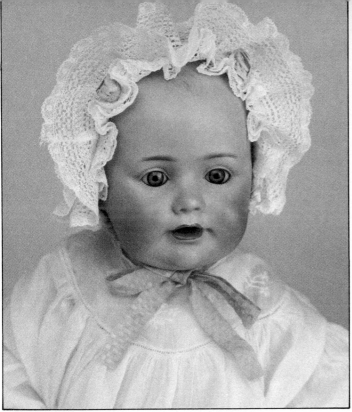

Bisque, German, 16 inches, marked *JDK 12*.
The hair on this doll is brushstroked. She has bright-blue sleep eyes and an open mouth with two teeth. This baby-doll series goes from number 8 to 16. Each doll is 2 inches larger than the previous one. The doll was modeled from the same baby as Hilda and there is a great similarity between them. Without the Hilda mark, the doll is not as valuable. This doll has the same body as the Hilda baby.

Bisque, German, Beschutz S. and Co., 22 inches, marked *LORI 1*.
Lori has blue sleep eyes, an open-closed mouth, a five-piece curved-limb baby body, and molded and painted blond hair. She is wearing an antique christening gown. This is a sought-after, high-priced baby doll. The composition body on this doll has more detail and is finer than any other baby doll. The body is plump and dimpled. For years, the maker of Lori-Baby has been unknown. A clue was found on the back of our large Lori's head. Incised in the hair color, just above the word LORI, is a large *D*. Lower on the neck is the round, green stamp of S and Co. There is a smaller baby doll with similar features with *D.V.* on the neck and the same green stamp of S and Co. The maker of the smaller doll is Davis and Voetch. Davis probably made Lori.

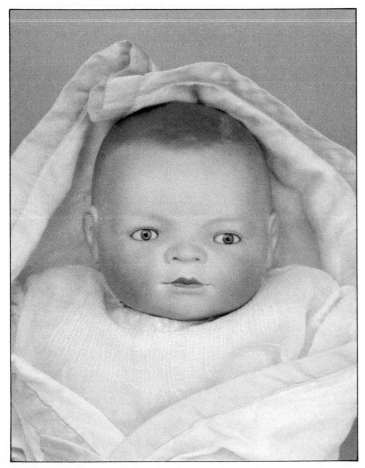

Bisque, German, Kestner, 17-1/2 inches, marked *Bye-Lo*.
This doll was copyrighted by Grace S. Putnam. She has blue sleep eyes, a cloth body, celluloid hands and molded, painted light-brown hair. These dolls were produced in 1923. She is wearing an old baby dress. This doll was called *The Million Dollar Baby Doll*.

Bisque, German, Character Children under 15 inches.
1. Kammer and Reinhardt 109, 101, 114, 111. 2. Schmidt boy doll, Kestner doll in high chair, two Kestner girls and K(star)R 111 sitting on the floor. All are under 15 inches high. 3. A.M. character doll.

Kammer and Reinhardt—K(star)R—made many character dolls. There are variations, such as glass eyes, painted eyes, wigs, molded hair, opened and closed months, and different sizes and painting. These are delightful dolls to collect. Two 11-inch K(star)R 114 dolls sold for $1,000 and $1,850. The only difference was the second one's brown eyes.

Collectors usually think dolls without a German mark were imported before 1891. The German mark was required after 1891, when the

Bisque, German, marked *K(star)R, Simon & Halbig 117-55.* This doll, called *Mein Liebling,* has an original blond wig and brown eyes. In 1982, this doll cost $4,500. She is one of the most beautiful German dolls made. The bisque is so smooth it glows. Painting is perfect. She is one of a character series made around 1912. There are at least three variations of this mold. Number 117 66 is the same mold, with larger eyes and slightly different painting. The same mold, 117 N (N for naughty), has an open mouth with teeth and flirty eyes. This means the eyes go from side to side when jiggled. They also sleep.

Bisque, German, 15 inches, marked *K(star)R 115 38.* *Philip* has molded hair and blue sleep eyes. The 1982 price was $1,400 at Theriault's.

Bisque, German, Heubach, Character dolls. These inexpensive dolls wear original gowns. This pair is worth more than two individual dolls.

law on imported dolls was changed. All dolls after that time were required to be marked for import. Collectors often think if a doll was not marked, it means it was made before 1891. This is not always the case. Some dolls had pasted-on stickers that came off. Some dolls were made for sale in Europe and were brought to America by travelers. Many dolls had already been made when the law went into effect and were not marked. Some dolls simply cannot be dated.

Bisque, German, Googly, 11 inches, marked *Einco.*
An unusual feature of *Valentine* is the lever that changes her eyes from one side to the other. She is a rare doll. Googlies are exciting to collect by themselves and are excellent investments. Googlies were not produced in large quantities, so they are good investments.

Bisque, German, Heubach, 13 inches, marked *Heubach Koppelsdorf, 318.7-0, A.H. Schalkay D.R.G.M.*
Elvia, the doll on the right, is a rare Googly, signed by the artist.

Googlies are also German-made. Most collectors like these dolls. Googlies are most notable for their wide-open eyes, with the pupil set or painted to the side. It's nice to have one or two in a collection.

Googlies are fun to collect by themselves. These dolls were not produced in large quantities, so don't pass them up as an investment. An unusual feature of some Heubach Googlies is a lever behind the ear that changes the eyes from one side to the other.

Bisque, German, Googly, 7-1/2 inches, marked *A.M. 232 and Heubach* in a square.
These dolls are dressed in charming costumes.

Bisque, German, Googly, 16 inches, marked _K(star)R,_ _Simon and Halbig 131._
This is a full view of the doll, showing her costume.

Close-up of the doll's face shows her googly eyes.

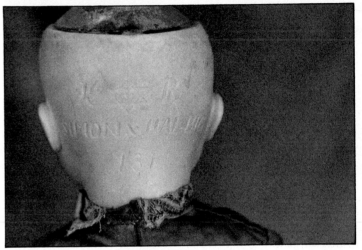

Back of the doll's head is marked.

Bisque, German, Googly, Armand Marseille.
A pair of A.M. Googlies.

Bisque, German, Googly, Kestner, 13 inches, marked _JDK_ _221 Gesgesch._
The Googly on the left has blue googly sleep eyes, an original mohair wig, jointed toddler composition body and an antique dress.

Bisque, German, Kestner, 14 inches, marked *165.5*.
The blue, googly sleep eyes, blond mohair wig and jointed composition body of this doll are original. She is wearing her original dress.

Bisque, French, SFBJ, 10 inches, marked *SFBJ 245 Paris*.
This doll has a cork body, composition arms and legs, glass eyes and a swivel head. Its costume was designed by Ruth Kleine. Not many French Googlies were made.

Bisque, German, Kestner, 11 inches, marked *163-2*.
Molded-hair Googlies were made between 1910 and 1915. This doll sold for $1,550 in 1981.

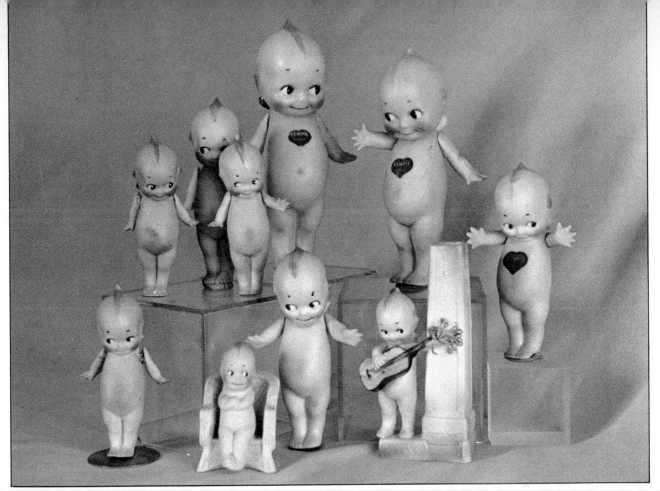

Bisque, Kewpie.
Action Kewpies are more sought after than plain-standing Kewpies. They have some accessory, such as a gun, umbrella or book. Some Kewpies are marked with a paper label with the words *Design Patent* in a circle. On the bottom, there is a copyright symbol. The Rose O'Neill signature is on the feet. These were the last authentic Kewpies to be made.

AMERICAN DOLLS

American bisque dolls are not popular because they are not beautiful. They are usually collected by people who only want to collect dolls made in the United States.

Most American-designed dolls were produced in Germany. Many of these dolls are excellent investments. They make a small, interesting collection. Some American-designed bisque dolls include Putnam's Million Dollar Bye-Lo, Averill dolls, Laughing Baby or Bonnie Babe, and the rare Grace Cory's molded-hair toddlers.

The Kewpies of Rose O'Neill are often a collection by themselves. There are other American dolls that make good investments. One method is to collect an artist's signed-dolls. Examples are Helen Jenson's Gladdie, Jean Orsini's all-bisque children, Oscar Hit's Googly, Grace Drayton's Dolly Dingle, Baby Bokay, Bernard Lipfert's Tynie Baby and others.

Bisque, Kewpie.
The *Kewpie Reader.* This is one of the more expensive action Kewpies. These dolls can cost from $50 to $350.

Bisque, American, 20 inches, marked *Baby Millie.*
This portrait-artist's baby doll was sculptured by Joyce Wolf in 1981. The accompanying tag reads "Sculptured as a tribute to Mildred Seeley for her contribution to doll making." This doll was done from baby pictures of me. The hands and feet are also molded to match old photos.

Collections of portrait dolls made by American artists should be included in the bisque category. Portrait dolls are made to resemble a particular person. They are original designs produced in limited numbers, with all work being done by the artist. Now on the market are bisque dolls of movie stars and other famous people. Portrait dolls have also been done of different children.

ALL-BISQUE DOLLS

All-bisque dolls, either French or German, are the miniatures of the doll world. Miniatures are under 8 inches high. Many of them were purchased from the candy counter for pennies.

Miniature dolls have a body and head made of bisque. Dolls with swivel heads, glass eyes, wigs and bare feet are sought by collectors. By the early 1980s, prices reached as high as $500 to $600, especially for French dolls. They are not usually dressed. These dolls can be displayed in a small space and dressed with tiny amounts of material.

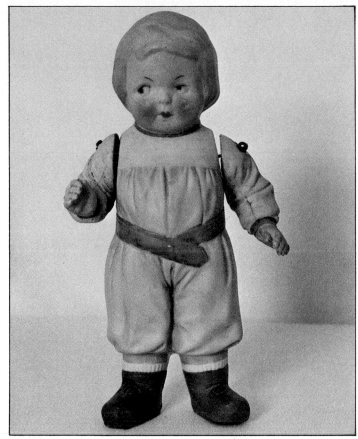

All-Bisque.
An all-bisque boy doll with jointed arms. He resembles the Drayton dolls with the side-turned eyes.

All-Bisque.
An all-bisque doll with jointed arms only.

All-Bisque, 4 and 5 inches.
These glass-eye, all-bisque dolls are dressed in old or original costumes. The dolls at the bottom center and bottom right have sleep eyes and open mouths with teeth. It is unusual in 4-inch and 5-inch dolls to find these details.

All-Bisque, German, 6 inches.
These two German all-bisque dolls at right are 6 inches high. They have jointed arms and legs are one piece. The boy has molded hair and the girl has a mohair wig. Both were recently dressed.

All-Bisque, French, 5-1/2 inches.
This all-bisque doll has jointed arms, one-piece legs and her original wig. She also has glass eyes.

All-Bisque, Kestner and Heubach, 12 inches.
Two unusually large, all-bisque baby dolls are shown at top right. The one with clothing is made by Kestner, the other by Heubach. Both are about 12 inches high.

All-Bisque, Googly.
All-bisque Googlies are fun to collect. There are glass-eye ones, like these at right, and ones with painted eyes. These dolls have original wigs and homemade clothing.

Miniature Googlies make excellent collector's dolls. They go up in value faster than other miniatures. All-bisque Googlies are fun to collect. There are glass-eye ones and painted ones.

All-bisque dolls with *molded clothing* are also collected. Molded clothing is clothing formed in the mold of the doll. All-bisque dolls were made in Germany, Japan, France and the United States. The Frozen Charlotte, an all-bisque doll with no joints, may have been made as early as 1840.

During the height of French doll making, most manufacturers made some all-bisque dolls. These sold for a low price and were usually unmarked. If you study these dolls, you may see resemblances between them and the faces of larger, more well-known dolls. These miniatures are not labeled and should be collected for the enjoyment of doll collecting.

A collection of dolls in original clothing, all under 2-1/2 inches. They are displayed under a low glass dome. The surface is a mirror.

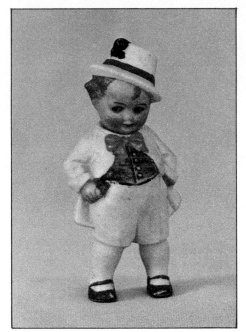

All-Bisque.
This is an all-bisque *nodder.* His head is loosely attached with elastic. He is only 3 inches high.

All-Bisque.
This is a group of all-bisque dolls with molded clothing. They range in size from 3 to 7 inches. Collections of this kind fit neatly into small cabinets.

Bisque, German, Googly, 11 inches, marked *172.*
An excellent example of a collectable, unmarked doll.

UNMARKED BISQUE DOLLS

Some bisque dolls have no markings on their head, shoulder or body. These dolls are called *unmarked bisque dolls.* The Long-Face Jumeau is an example of a head marked with only a number. This doll is identified by the way it looks. Its face is longer than other Jumeau dolls.

Some Bru doll heads are also unmarked. The head may have been removed from a marked shoulder plate and put on a different body. A shoulder plate is the top shoulder part of the doll that has an indentation for the neck to fit into.

There is a group of beautiful closed-mouth, unmarked dolls with a French appearance. The value of this group is increasing rapidly. These dolls are marked IX, X, XI, 14, 16 and so on. Some people call them Kestners because they sometimes have plaster pates.

Bisque, 27 inches, marked *16.*
This doll has a closed mouth. She is wearing an ash-brown, human-hair replacement wig. Her pink silk costume was designed and made by Helen Kramer.

Bisque, 16 inches.
The doll at top right wears her original sheepskin wig and original clothing. She has a leather body.

Bisque, French clowns, Lanternier et Cie., 10-1/2 inches, marked *LC* **in an anchor.**
SFBJ Company made bisque clowns about 1910. *Ladies Home Journal* showed some of these in December of that year. These dolls are untinted white bisque, with black-glass eyes. Feet and legs are weighted. Clowns are fun to collect. These clowns were reasonably priced and purchased in 1982 at a Scottsdale, Arizona auction. They add variety, color and enjoyment to doll collecting. They are not good investment dolls, because there is no precedent to decide their value.

Bisque, German, Simon and Halbig, 6-1/2 inches.
This is an Oriental-looking doll with black sleep eyes, an original black wig, molded slippers with heels, one-piece arms and legs, and original clothing.

Bisque, German, 9-1/2 inches, marked *390, A 12/OXM*.
She has gray-blue eyes, an open mouth with teeth, composition one-piece arms and legs, and original clothing. These German dolls, under 10 inches, make a worthwhile collection. Each would probably cost less than $200.

BISQUE DOLLS IN ORIGINAL COSTUMES

Bisque dolls in original clothing, both French and German, are valuable to collectors. To own a doll in original clothing is an asset. Dolls in completely original condition are referred to as *mint* in ads and auction catalogs. Don't pay for a doll advertised "with original costume and in perfect condition" unless you see it. There are few available and the purchase price is high.

Dolls with even part of their original clothing, such as dresses, underclothes, hats or shoes, are valuable. Old shoes may sell for as much as $100 for a pair marked Bru.

At one auction, several dolls were sold without clothing. Later, complete sets of old clothing to fit the dolls were auctioned separately. Some-times an experienced collector with a sharp eye will find clothing has been divided among several dolls.

REPRODUCTION BISQUE DOLLS

As you become more knowledgable about dolls, you will detect which dolls are reproductions and which ones are antiques. Most reproduction dolls are identified by their painting. Only the best doll artists can paint feathered eyebrows and fine lashes like old dolls. The following points will help you determine if a doll is a reproduction doll.

● Compare the painting to the painting on an old doll. Look for the artist's markings on the back of the reproduction doll's head.

Bisque, German, 10 inches, marked *1894 AM 6/0 DEP*.
Boy doll with blue eyes, an open mouth with four teeth, and one-piece arms and legs. His original clothing is nailed to his body.

Bisque, German, 9 inches, marked *Germany, 7/0*.
She has a dark-brown body, one-piece arms and legs, molded yellow shoes, dark-brown eyes and open mouth with four teeth. Her original wig and costume make this doll fun to collect.

● Colored bisque inside the head almost always indicates a reproduction doll. Old dolls were made of white bisque. Heubach made some dolls with pink bisque. Most artists today paint on precolored bisque, not white bisque.

● Color, quality, pitted-in dirt and small imperfections in the bisque usually indicate an antique doll. Use a strong magnifying glass to check these points.

● Reproduction heads usually have a rim around the neck edge to protect them from warping during firing. Most old French dolls have heads that are cut off with no rim or collar around the top of the head.

● Reproduction heads are clean inside. Because of age, there is usually some dirt inside old bisque heads. A reproduction head is always smaller than the original—at least 16% smaller. This is caused by the shrinkage of porcelain.

● Check key items on the body. A reproduction composition body has a different feel. It "gives" a bit when pinched. An old body does not. A new body is a uniform color throughout. Paint is usually worn off someplace on an old body.

● New bodies are usually strung together by inserting an iron washer into the lower leg and hands. Old dolls have a mounted hook in the leg to hold elastic. New bodies don't have wooden inserts in the joints, but old bodies usually do.

● Paint on new bodies is usually latex, with a plastic coating that can be washed. Old bodies have a water-soluble finish. They can only be cleaned with wax.

Best of Bisque Dolls

Certain bisque dolls are the best to purchase for investment. However, there are not many of these dolls available. Their workmanship and scarcity make them valuable.

The best bisque dolls are expensive to buy. This chapter discusses these dolls in detail so collectors may learn as much as possible before making a large investment.

SELLING PRICES

At right is a list of prices of dolls sold from 1978 to 1981. Prices given for a particular doll, such as the E.J. Jumeau, are not for the same doll sold three different times. They are different dolls of the same type sold in those years. Dolls are all similar in size. Clothing and wear on each doll varied. It's interesting to see how prices change.

SELLING PRICES			
27" E.J. Jumeau	1978-$2,400	1980-$3,800	1981-$7,700
16" Schoenhut	1970-$35	1978-$125	1980-$500
23" China	1974-$35	1978-$160	1981-$450
17-1/2" Bye-Lo	1970-$135	1979-$225	1981-$575
23" Lori	1979-$500	1980-$600	1981-$2,900
9" French all-bisque	1969-$25	1979-$200	1981-$1,200
16" Chase cloth	1970-$35	1978-$80	1981-$450
19" Lenci felt	1970-$40	1979-$1,800	1981-$1,850
21" K(star)R 114	1969-$300	1979-$900	1981-$4,400
16" XI Unmarked doll	1970-$300	1980-$1,100	1981-$2,300
6" Dollhouse doll	1970-$25	1979-$65	1981-$550

Bisque, French, Jumeau.
The Jumeau at left is sitting on a hand-carved Raiker horse. Dolls displayed in the home add charm and brightness.

Bisque, marked *XI*.
A bisque doll marked only with *XI* is shown at top. She is a choice doll.

Bisque, French, Schmitt, marked with crossed hammers and *SCH*.
The doll on the left has brown paperweight eyes, a blond sheepswool wig and original clothing. Her clothing, shoes and hat have original Paris labels. She is 15 inches high. The doll on the right has blue-lined paperweight eyes, a marked body and antique costume and shoes. The shoes are antique, but not original. She is 16 inches high.

Bisque, French, Schmitt, 15 inches, marked with crossed hammers and *SCH*.
This doll is wearing an antique satin skirt, silk top, antique shoes and bonnet. The clothes are probably not original.

LIST OF VALUABLE DOLLS

Some dolls are classed as "most valuable" by name alone. This does not consider size, condition or other value points that may affect price. A summary of top-name dolls to collect appears below, listed in order of value.

Albert Marque doll
H-doll
A. Thuillier doll
Huret doll
Bru doll
Jumeau doll
Steiner doll
The following dolls are about equal in value:
F. Gauthier dolls
Schmitt dolls
German character dolls
Certain Googlies

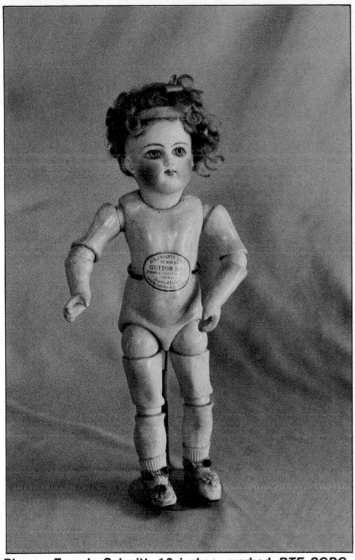

Bisque, French, Schmitt, 12 inches, marked *BTE SGDG 3/0.*
The body of this doll is marked with crossed hammers, plus a shop sticker. Her blue eyes, pale bisque, original hair and clothing make her a mint doll.

This is the same doll shown dressed. She could be collected with the under-14-inch dolls. She is an excellent find, but expensive.

The value of top dolls does not remain the same. Each feature of a doll moves it up or down the scale. Beauty, rarity, condition and other factors must be considered. A broken, bedraggled A. Thuillier doll, also referred to as an *A.T.*, is less valuable than a lovely Bru doll in excellent condition. A K(star)R doll in original costume is probably more valuable than a Jumeau doll with a bad crack.

Judgment must be developed by the collector. Some dolls are fads. They are highly priced today, but their future value is uncertain. An example of a fad doll is a celebrity doll or a cartoon character. In the future, no one may know or care who these dolls represent.

In 1981, an Oriental Bru sold for the highest recorded auction price of $16,500. An Albert Marque sold for $36,000, the record price for a dealer sale. The highest private sale was $28,000 for an H-doll.

Investing in dolls can be profitable. In recent years, dolls have increased in value or held steady. Investing in dolls is a speculative venture and must be done with care and forethought.

Bisque, French, Marque, 22 inches.
We named this doll *Alyce*. She has pierced ears, bisque arms to the elbow, brown eyes and blond hair. Alyce is in her original silk taffeta dress and smocked velvet bonnet bearing a Paris label. This is one of the world's most valuable dolls. Her head mold was not made for a large production. It was made in five pieces, instead of two. Her body is tall and thin, with side joints. Shoes are marked.

ALBERT MARQUE DOLLS

Rare Albert Marque dolls are normally the top investment value. They are the most expensive dolls you can buy. In 1981, one in extremely poor condition sold for $36,000. It was the record price for a doll up to that time. These dolls have never been sold at public auction because they are very rare.

Until 1981, little was known about Marque dolls, not even the maker's first name. In making molds of the Marque head, we were convinced the dolls were not made by a doll maker, but by a sculptor. We began doing a lot of research on French sculptors and their works.

We consulted *Dictionnaire des Peintres, Sculpteurs, Dessinateurs, et Graveurs*, by Benezit. We found that Albert Marque was a Parisian sculptor born in France in 1872. The book listed some of his awards and sculptures. In the June 1939 edition of *Beaux Arts*, we found his obituary. In the article he was called "this friend of small children."

We believe most Albert Marque dolls came to this country from the shop of Margaine Lacroix. Her labels are in all the old costumes on Marque dolls that we have found.

Bisque, French, Marque, 22 inches.
André has blue paperweight eyes and red hair. His costume
has a label in the green-velvet, silk-lined jacket.

Mme. Lacroix did the beautiful costuming on many Marque dolls. Five dolls, perhaps more, were dressed as queens of France. Others were dressed as French peasant children. The first authenticated date on these dolls was their importation directly from Mme. Lacroix to the Carnegie Museum on April 13, 1916.

All Marque dolls are 22 inches high. They were all made from the same mold—both boys and girls. They have the same brown-leather pointed shoes. The dolls have brown or blue paperweight eyes.

The sculpture of Marque dolls is different from other dolls. Features are sharp, elflike and more defined than other dolls. Heads are done in five-piece molds, not two pieces like other dolls. The hands and lower arms are porcelain.

The body is tall and thin, with a shape that is different from bodies made by other doll makers.

There are two reasons collectors should be aware of these dolls. You might run into a Marque doll, owned by someone since childhood and not recognized as a collector's prize. Also, Marque dolls may now be purchased as reproductions. Inexperienced collectors should know if they are buying a reproduction.

My two Marque dolls, a peasant boy and girl, are dressed in original costumes with labels. They were purchased in the early 1940s from Harriet Miller, who lived in Arlington, Vermont. Mrs. Miller owned an antique shop and spent part of each year in France. She located 10 pairs of Marques in a warehouse in Canada.

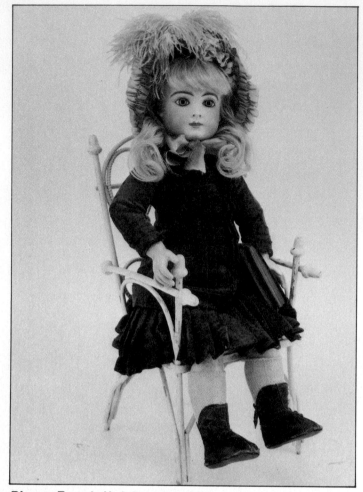

Bisque, French, H-doll, marked *1H.*
As with many early dolls, *Bèbè Halo* has pierced, applied ears. Her porcelain head is pressed, rather than poured. Her unusual blue eyes, original costume and wooden body, with its detailed modeling of toes and hands, make her a collector's doll. H-dolls, though not as expensive as Marque dolls, are considered the most beautiful dolls. They are highly desired by established collectors.

This picture shows more detail in Bébé Halo's face.

MYSTERY DOLL

There is a mystery doll marked only with a size number and an *H*. No one knows the maker of this rare, beautiful doll. They are so scarce that only a few collectors have them. This doll ranges in price between the Marque and the A.T. dolls. In 1982, an H-doll sold for $28,000. It had its original body, wig and costume.

H-dolls, though not as expensive as Marques, are considered the most beautiful and consummate dolls.

The face shape, body and workmanship of an H-doll do not resemble that of any other doll. The pierced, applied ears are a unique design. They are made separately from the head and attached after the head is removed from the mold.

Heads on H-dolls were made of the finest translucent white porcelain. They were pressed into the mold rather than poured. This is verified when the wig and pate are removed. If you run your fingers over the inside, you can feel ridges from the pressing. Pressing was used for making heads before pouring became popular. Lips and nose are filled with porcelain. They do not have the even thickness obtained by pouring.

Lips are painted a delicate color, with a little white space between them. They are accented with a slightly darker shade. Eyelashes are fine and black. Brows are soft, with feathering. A soft blush, or rosy color, covers cheeks, backs of hands and other parts of the doll's body to give it a soft glow. The same color is shaded over the eyes.

Bisque, French, H-doll, 25 inches, marked 4H.
Seeley's Jewel. She has her original body, wig, costume and shoes. This is considered one of the world's most beautiful dolls. H-dolls are old, made of the finest material and well-crafted. They are rare and have universal appeal.

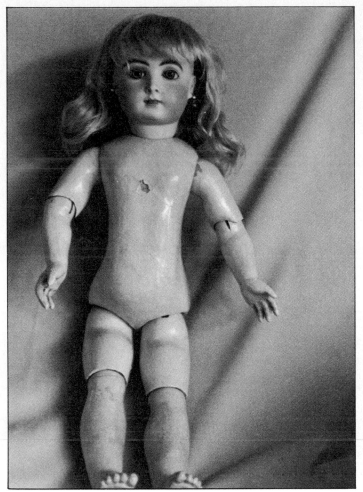

Bisque, French, H-doll, marked 1H.
Study the parts of this H-doll, Bébé Halo. She has lovely eyes and a beautiful face. If you find one, you will be able to recognize it.

The body of an H-doll differs from other dolls. Wrists are straight, with hands gracefully positioned. Each nail is long, narrow and well-shaped. Toes are shaped on the top and on the underside, with shaped nails. The torso has a shape and waistline. Joints are smooth and work well.

All these dolls apparently had blue eyes. The blue varies from light blue to teal-blue, with radiating white lines. The iris is circled with black. They are unlike the eyes of any other doll.

Our doll, *Bébé Halo,* is 19 inches high. H-dolls are also found up to 25 inches high. They are works of art and worth the effort of finding them.

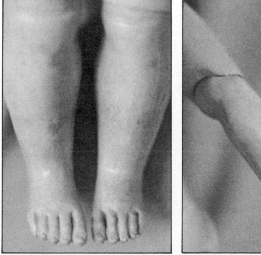

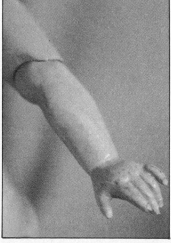

A close-up of the Bébé Halo's lower legs and feet.

The arm and hand of Bébé Halo.

Bisque, French, A. Thuillier, 13-1/2 inches, marked *A.T. 3*.
This A.T. has blue-lined paperweight eyes, leather body and feet, bisque lower arms, a shoulder plate marked A.T. 3, a mohair wig and pierced ears. Her costume was made by Dr. Vivian Iob from old material.

A. THUILLIER DOLLS

Dolls by A. Thuillier, also called A.T.s, may be the best examples of dolls with universal appeal. These dolls are a better value than a Bru doll. They are better because they are rarer, sometimes older—made in the 1880s—and may be more beautiful.

These dolls are sought by collectors and do not usually appear at auctions. In 1981, a No. 3 A.T., about 14 inches high on an unknown body, sold for over $7,000 at auction. We paid $6,000 for ours in 1980. Our doll is in perfect condition,

on an authentic leather body with bisque hands. Also in 1981, a 16-inch A.T. sold for $15,500 at auction. It had a questionable body and poor proportions.

Well-made A.T.s are works of art. They are a joy to own and look at. But you must be careful. A.T.s with open mouths and teeth are usually poor quality. They have the appearance of having been made by a different company. Bisque is poor and painting is bad. See an A.T. before you buy it.

Bisque, French, Huret.
This Huret doll was purchased at auction. Her original costume is a bit threadbare, but she is still a collector's doll.

A close-up of the same doll. Notice the unusual shape of her face.

HURET DOLLS

The Huret doll is another rare, high-priced doll. Any Huret doll is an excellent investment for collectors. Huret dolls have unusual faces and construction. For highest value, a Huret should be on its original wood-jointed body. No other wooden doll body is like it.

A Huret body may be found with a head other than a Huret. This may happen because the original Huret head was broken or Huret sold his doll bodies to other manufacturers.

The Huret doll head has unusual features that give it a different look. It cannot be confused with a Bru, Jumeau or other French doll head. Construction is also different. A 2-inch porcelain stem on the base of the neck goes down into the body.

The Huret doll was made with painted or glass eyes. Value is equal for both types. The Huret doll is valuable because of its rarity and uniqueness. The Huret's rarity make it a prized possession for collectors.

Bisque, French, Bru, 11 inches, marked *Bru Jne 2*.
The original mohair wig and original silk-and-lace dress were found on this doll. She has beautiful brown eyes and perfect hands.

This is a close-up of the same doll. She is in nearly perfect condition.

BRU DOLLS

The right Bru doll is a good investment. For a few years these dolls doubled in value each year. Then they more than tripled in value. There is a difference in the quality of Brus. Older ones are finer and more beautiful.

The quality of Brus marked with an R, made after 1892, is different than those made earlier. Those with an R have thick, shiny eyebrows and lashes that are too long. These features are often found on dolls with composition bodies. We did not buy a Bru with an R until we bought our Kissing Bru because they lacked the appeal of older Brus.

The late Brus with an R, sleep eyes or an open mouth seem less appealing. Because of the Bru name, their prices are high. Beginning collectors seeking their first Bru often buy these dolls. The early Nursing Bru, with its open mouth, is an exception. It may be a good buy. Look for Brus with fine faces.

The value points on Bru dolls are different from those of other dolls, mainly because of their construction. Most collectors start at the bottom with the poorest Bru and work up. Brus in good condition are not easy to find.

Bisque, French, Bru.
The Kissing Bru is in original costume.

The Kissing Bru is shown undressed. She is in mint condition and adds historic value to a collection.

Bisque, French, Bru.
A collection of 11 Bru dolls that span many years. It is fun to compare numbers, sizes and faces in this group. A quality collection should have at least one of these dolls. 1. Bru with crescent. 2. Incised *Bru Jne 10*. 3. Black Bru, *Jne 7*. 4. Bru *Jne 6*. 5. Bru *Jne 6*. 6. Head and shoulder plate Bru *Jne 5*. 7. Bru *Jne 4*. 8. Nursing Bru, incised Bru *Jne 4*. 9. Marked 3 and circle and dot. 10. Kissing Bru. 11. No marks.

You may find Brus on composition bodies. Shoulder plates might have been broken or leather bodies lost. Heads have been saved and put on composition bodies. Our Bru Jne 10 is on a composition body. She may have been on that body originally.

The middle class of Brus is usually an excellent buy. These are Brus with a shoulder plate with bisque arms and wooden legs. This type of doll has a leather body to the knees. Bisque arms are jointed at the elbow. There is usually a leather-covered metal piece in the upper arm. The metal piece ends in a wooden ball that fits into the bisque shoulder plate. This allows the arm to be lifted at the shoulder. The wooden leg is jointed to the upper leg, giving it some movement. Wooden legs often have peeling paint. Sometimes toes are broken off. The shoulder plate of this doll is usually open under the arms. A desirable variation is wooden arms. Bisque legs are also desirable and unusual.

The oldest construction of Bru dolls is a full-leather body with leather legs and feet. Leather comes down below the elbow. The bisque arm is cut off and inserted into the leather halfway between the wrist and elbow. The bisque shoulder plate is closed under the arm. These bodies are often crippled and warped, somewhere between

Bisque, French, Bru.
1. 15 inches, marked *Bru Jne 4. Violette* has brown paper-weight eyes, a leather body, wooden legs and bisque arms. Her body label is still attached. She is wearing a blond mohair wig and her costume is antique material. 2. 23-1/2 inches, marked *Bru Jne 10. Rosemary* is dressed in an antique satin costume. She has a composition body. 3. Marked *Bru Jne 5.* This little doll has wooden legs and bisque arms.

Bisque, French, Bru, marked *Bru Jne 11.*
Tennie has a marked shoulder plate and brown paperweight eyes. She has a leather body and feet, and bisque hands. She is dressed in her original silk brocade dress and coral necklace.

a sitting and a standing position. A good one is worth what you have to pay for it. You can determine the age of a Bru by its body construction.

Brus should have depth to the eyes. Eyes should match. Check inside the head to judge whether eyes are original. If the eyes have been reset or changed, old and new plaster lines are usually not the same. Sometimes unevenness of dirt indicates changed eyes.

Eyes in the oldest Brus, on an all-leather body, have a special depth and color, especially blue eyes. They make the doll beautiful. Looking from the side, the eyes have a clear bulge.

Eyes in the head on a composition body may have been changed. Check inside the head.

Study the bisque. Bisque can be bad in any doll, but poor quality is more apt to occur in later ones. Bisque should be smooth in a Bru, with no rough spots or tiny blisters. Most bisque dolls have a few brown, iron-oxide specks.

A bisque head on an all-leather body was usually pressed in the mold, rather than poured. You can determine this by looking inside and running your finger over the surface. It will be full of fine ridges.

Bisque, French, Bru, marked *Bru Jne 5*.
Fiona has blue paperweight eyes, a white line between lips, a leather body and wooden legs. She wears her original human-hair wig, a reproduction silk dress and antique boots.

Bisque, French, Bru, marked *Bru Jne 5*.
Freckles has a few brown iron-oxide specks on her face. There is a paper label on the torso of this doll. She is wearing an auburn wig and has blue paperweight eyes, a leather body, bisque arms and wooden legs.

Hold the head to the light. It will have an uneven thickness. The nose and lips will be dark. The rest of the head will be translucent.

We believe all Brus had pierced ears. It is delightful to find one with original earrings. The only earrings we have found are turquoise glass.

Study the painting on the doll. The brows on Brus are not identical. On early Brus, brows are soft, dull and pleasant. If the brows and lashes are heavy, shiny and harsh, the doll should have an R after the *Bru Jne*. It is a later Bru and may be on a composition body.

As you study painted-on lips and lashes, you will learn if they are done well. The color on cheeks varies on older Brus. Newer ones are more highly blushed.

Labels are desirable. It is good if there is a paper label across the leather chest. This indicates the doll has not been taken apart many times. You also have a reference to check date and other things.

As for other markings, the numbers on the back of the head and the shoulder plate should match. A Bru *Jne 7* should have a 7 on the shoul-

Bisque, French, Bru.
These dolls show two different Bru bodies. The doll on the right has leather legs and her shoulder plate is open under the arms. The one on the left has wooden legs and a shoulder plate closed under the arms. The doll on the right was made earlier then the one on the left.

der plate. The oldest markings seem to be the crescent, and the circle and dot.

Bisque hands are important. It is hard to find Brus with perfect hands. Many have missing fingers or fingertips. The price you pay should reflect this. With the exception of Brus with composition bodies, all Bru hands are from the same mold.

Consider the wig. Apparently all Bru wigs were of similar design. Most were fine-quality mohair. Some older Brus had lambskin wigs.

Front hair on the wig was pulled back and up to the top of the head. It was fastened and ended in low curls. Soft, short bangs or fringe came across the forehead. The back and sides were gently curled. A few old Bru wigs still exist.

Preserve old wigs when possible. An original wig is the best style for the face. It calls attention to the beautiful eyes. Value increases if an old wig can be salvaged.

Old clothing, underclothing, corsets, socks and Bru-marked shoes are important in assessing the value of a doll. Original Bru costumes or bonnets are valuable.

Bisque, French, Bru, marked *Bru Jne 8*.
Cherish has markings on her shoulder plate and head. Her chest label is still partially attached. Her hands are perfect and her body is straight-cut leather, including her feet. She has beautiful blue paperweight eyes. To add to her perfection, she is wearing her original wig and dress.

A superior Bru has a straight leather body and legs, a closed bisque shoulder plate, a bisque head with deep, paperweight eyes, perfect hands, an antique mohair wig, original marking on the bottom of shoes, old undergarments, original fancy costume and a bonnet with a label. If all these are in acceptable condition, the doll will demand top price.

Brus cost a lot of money. They are worth the price because no more dolls will be made. Old dolls must be passed down to the next generation of collectors.

Tiny Brus are hard to find. Their prices are higher than larger Brus that are similar. Tiny Bru dolls take little space to display.

If you can't find or afford the top value, you may have to buy what you can find. Later you can exchange it for a better doll.

Bru made a doll called the Kissing Bru. Directions say to raise the right arm up to the shoulder, turn the head toward it, pull the cord and the doll will throw a kiss.

My Kissing Bru, shown on page 79, has original underclothing made of stiff, lace-trimmed gauze. There is a little hole in the dress where the cord that works the kiss-throwing arm passes through the clothing. The crude 6-piece papier-mâché body is still in excellent condition. The marked shoes are also well-preserved. The face on this doll does not look like a Bru, possibly due to its squinty eyes. The hair is the fine, soft hair of a small child. The doll cost 97 cents in the United States when it was made. The inexpensive, poorly made Bru shows the difference in Bru production. The doll will never increase in value or be a good investment.

Bisque, French, Jumeau.
The L-Jumeau was made for the Louvre Department Store in Paris, France.

Bisque, French, Jumeau, marked *Tête Jumeau*.
Most collectors want at least one Jumeau. They come in many sizes, ranging from 10 to 40 inches.

Bisque, French, Jumeau.
The doll at bottom right is named *Lyric* and she is a choice Jumeau. Jumeaus in original costumes are not often found.

JUMEAU DOLLS

The doll-making firm of Jumeau was established in the middle of the 19th century by Pierre Françoise Jumeau. The business was carried on by Emile Jumeau. When Jumeau began to make dolls, he used German and Gauthier heads. In 1879, Jumeau started making everything for the dolls in his own factory. He built a reputation for fine dolls.

Jumeau dolls are always a good investment. Jumeaus marked with an E.J. or Déposé, or the Long-Face Jumeaus are the most valuable. *E.J.* stands for Emile Jumeau. *Déposé* means the doll was registered. *Long-Face Jumeaus* had a longer face than most other Jumeaus. There is variation in Jumeau dolls, but they make an interesting, valuable collection.

There are some rare character Jumeaus. One sold for $12,000 at auction in 1981. This is more than any regular Jumeau would cost. Signed E.J.s are also expensive. Most of them are beautiful.

Bisque, French, Jumeau, 21 inches, marked *Déposé Jumeau 9*.
Carrie has blue eyes, a white line between her lips, applied ears and large hands.

This type of Jumeau is often referred to as the *Incised Jumeau*. This means the name Jumeau was indented into the doll's head. Features on this doll, such as the eye cutting, the huge applied ears and the size of the arms and hands, are not as refined as on later dolls.

The Long-Face Jumeau is a top collector's choice. Be sure unmarked heads are on Jumeau-marked bodies or Simonne bodies. You must decide from the modeling whether or not it has a long face. It is sometimes difficult for a beginner to do this without another doll for comparison.

Some heads on Jumeau-marked bodies are *Portrait Jumeaus*. These dolls were made to look like a particular person. They are good collectors' dolls. Any portrait-type dolls is an excellent investment. On some older Jumeaus, the bisque was pressed into the mold, instead of poured. Nose and mouth indentations on the inside of the head are filled. Ears are made in a separate mold and applied to the porcelain before firing.

Some Jumeaus are referred to as *Incised Jumeaus*. This means the name Jumeau was carved or indented into the doll's bisque head. Some Jumeaus were stamped instead of incised.

The best way to judge Jumeaus is by the fineness of the bisque, the beauty of paperweight

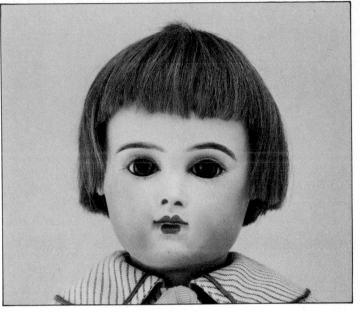

Above is a close-up of Chadwick.

Bisque, French, Jumeau, 22 inches, marked *Jumeau 9 Déposé.*
At left is *Chadwick,* one of only a few Jumeau boy dolls made. They appear to be an afterthought, because they have pierced ears.

Bisque, French, Jumeau.
This is a Portrait Jumeau. Her unmarked head is on a stamped Jumeau body. Portrait Jumeaus usually have a more almond-shape eye than later Jumeaus.

Bisque, French, Jumeau, 15 inches, marked *L4.*
Bèbè Louvre has blue paperweight eyes, a marked composition, body, and an old or original dress and bonnet. These dolls, with several different markings but all with an *L,* were made for the Louvre Department Store in Paris. They are good investments. These dolls have a pensive look and come in different sizes.

Bisque, French, Jumeau, 18 inches.
This doll has blue eyes, a marked body and a human-hair wig. This doll and the one at right have the same head and body markings, but Bébé Peggy has a heavy body and large head. The other doll has jointed wrists and a leaner body. Her head is smaller in proportion to her body.

Bisque, French, Jumeau, 20 inches.
Bébé Peggy has blue paperweight eyes, a marked Jumeau body and a brown, human-hair wig.

eyes and the markings. All the Jumeaus we have found have pierced ears. The Long-Face Jumeaus, the E.J.s and the Incised Jumeaus have applied ears. The bodies on these have straight or unbroken wrists and large hands. Bodies are often marked. These dolls are readily available, so you shouldn't have to buy a cracked or put-together one.

Most Jumeau bodies are stamped with *1878 Paris Exposition, Medaille d'Or.* This does not mean that particular body was made in 1878. Jumeau used the mark on *all* bodies made after 1878. Some shoes also are dated, but this does not date the doll. The same shoes were used for many years. Shoes could have been switched from doll to doll.

Threaded Jumeau eyes have *yeux fibres*, which are lines running from outside the edge of the iris to the pupil. They are considered the finest quality. Sometimes in descriptions they are referred to as *lined eyes*.

Many people like Jumeaus with *feathered* eyes. These eyes are a deeper color and have a little feathering deep down. The feathering is found only in blue or gray-green eyes, not brown eyes.

Jumeaus were dolls that wealthy children played with. Few dolls are found in original cos-

Bisque, French, Jumeau.
Jumeaus give variety to a collection. In this picture are a Portrait Jumeau, an *L*, three Têtes and an Incised Jumeau.

tumes. Most dolls were elaborately dressed after they were made. Some were sold in chemises and dressed by the purchaser.

Original costumes and shoes on Jumeaus are valuable. If an original costume doesn't come with the doll, don't expect to find one that fits. The doll will have to wear a reproduction dress. We have only one costume we are positive is original with the doll. This is worn by our doll named *Lyric*.

The painting on later Jumeaus is different from earlier dolls. The mouth is redder and eyeshadow is amber-rust. Bottom lashes go straight down. Brows are three strokes of brown. Cheeks are highly colored. The bisque is dense. It is not difficult to see how Jumeaus have changed. High standards for bisque and excellent production methods were sacrificed to make less-expensive dolls in larger quantities.

Our collection has an assortment of Jumeau dolls, including Incised, Long Face and Stamped. But we wanted a good late-model Jumeau. To make our collection more complete, we sought a *Princess Elizabeth*. This doll was made in the 1930s, in the image of young Princess Elizabeth of Great Britain.

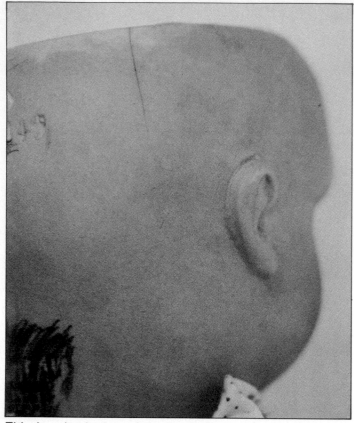

This is a back view of the head of our *Princess Elizabeth* Jumeau. Note the hairline crack not mentioned in the catalog.

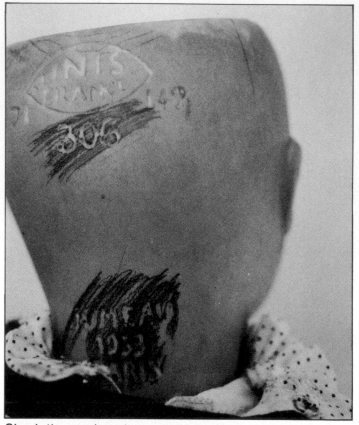

Check the numbers here with the catalog description given in the text. You can never be too careful when buying at auction.

French, Bisque, Jumeau, marked *Unis France 71 149 306, Jumeau 1933, Paris.*
This portrait of *Princess Elizabeth* is an example of a late-bisque doll.

A Princess Elizabeth Jumeau came up at auction. It seemed to be what we needed for a late-example Jumeau. At a distance she looked good. The auction catalog description read, "generally excellent, somewhat coarse bisque, incised *Unis France 71 149 309 Jumeau 1938 Paris*. Portrait doll of young Princess Elizabeth."

After close examination, our description would be, "Marked *Unis France 71 149 306 Jumeau 1933 Paris*. Old, black 3/4-inch hairline (very small) crack down back of head. Replaced upper legs and new hands. Eyes reset or replaced. Head appears to have had sleep eyes."

Her costume was attractive. The long, eyelet-trimmed drawers had a drawstring in the top. The dress, probably made recently, was an old-print fabric by Concord Fabrics, Inc. Her felt coat was trimmed with the same fabric. Her wig was probably new. Although this doll differed from the catalog description, I still bought her. But it does point out the fact that you must be careful buying at auctions.

The painting of this Jumeau doll is different from most Jumeaus. The mouth is redder, eyeshadow is amber-rust, bottom lashes go straight down, brows are three strokes of brown, cheeks are highly colored and the bisque is dense.

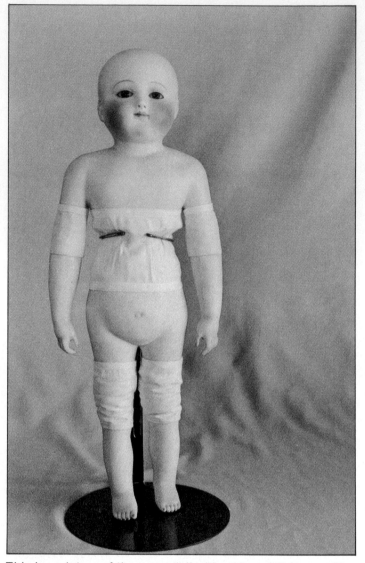

Bisque, French, Steiner, 21 inches.
Penelope has a blond mohair wig and cobalt-blue eyes.

This is a picture of the same doll without her clothing or wig, so you can see her bisque parts. She has the old Motschmann-type body. Her head and shoulders are in one piece. Her lower arms are attached with cloth strips. The midsection of the body is cloth. The hip section and lower legs are porcelain. She is a fine example of an early Steiner.

STEINER DOLLS

The Jules Nicholas Steiner Company is one of the oldest doll-making companies. It began producing dolls in 1855. The company made many different faces. Steiner dolls are an excellent investment.

The open-mouth Steiner, with a double row of pointed teeth, the closed-mouth bébés, and later Steiners are all good investments. The Kicking Steiner, Walking Steiner, Motschmann-type Steiner, Bergoin and wire-eye Steiners are sought for historical interest, beauty and value. The label of the Steiner Company—a girl with banner—was not placed on bodies until after 1889.

The term *Motschmann-type* means a doll made with leather or fabric inserts to facilitate

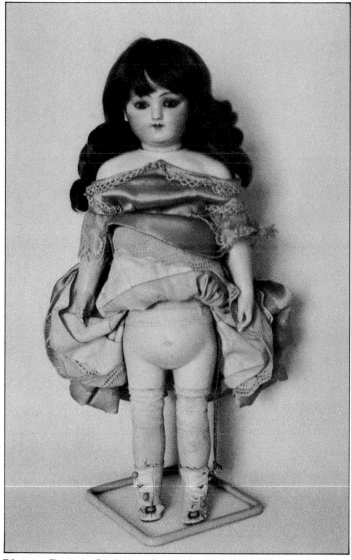

Bisque, French, Steiner, 16-1/2 inches, Motschmann-type.
She has an open mouth with pointed teeth, swivel head, auburn hair, antique pink satin dress and pink leather boots. Motschmann-type dolls are enjoyable to collect but few are found. Some are dressed in white cotton baby dresses, but this one was dressed as a child. Some have squeeze-box voices.

Bisque, French, Steiner, 23 inches, marked *Steiner, Paris, FA. 11.*
This doll has a seven-piece Steiner body, blue paperweight eyes, braided auburn hair and a soft blue-dotted silk antique dress.

movement. Motschmann patented this type of doll in Germany in 1857. Motschmann-type dolls are enjoyable to collect. There are only a few available today. Some were originally dressed in white cotton baby dresses. Some have squeeze-box voices.

Most Steiners have a purple cardboard *pate,* instead of the usual French cork pate. A pate is the piece of cardboard or cork that covers the top of an open head. Steiner also used purple paint as an undercoat on composition bodies. To find this, look in a joint where outside paint has worn off.

The fingers and toes on Steiner dolls are unusual. Fingers are about the same length. Sometimes the big toe is separate. Later Steiners had a jointed wrist. Smaller dolls had fingers joined together. Steiner also made a few black or mulatto dolls. They are lovely, but are difficult to find.

Bisque, French, Steiner, 13-1/2 inches, marked *B.S. 6. D. G. J. Bergoin, SUGG.*
All wire-eye Steiners have marked ceramic eyes with a glass inset. This composition body is marked Steiner. She is wearing an old satin costume and a blond, human-hair wig.

Bisque, French, Steiner, 23 inches, marked *StEC5;* over the ear *J. Steiner, BSGDG, J. Bergoin, SUGG.*
She has a marked Steiner body and wire eyes.

This is the same doll, showing her original, embroidered white dress. The lever for moving her eyes is behind her left ear.

Bisque, French, Steiner.
A rare black-brown Steiner doll.

Bisque, French, Gauthier, 16 inches, marked *F.C.G.*
She has blue paperweight eyes, a blond mohair wig, a reproduction dress and antique Bru shoes.

Bisque, French, Gauthier, 16 inches, marked *F.C.G.*
The blue paperweight eyes, original earrings and cream-silk reproduction dress make this doll worth collecting.

FRANÇOISE GAUTHIER DOLLS

Dolls by Françoise Gauthier are interesting, with their large eyes. They are sometimes referred to as F.G. dolls. Earlier dolls had an F.G. imprinted high up under the hair. Some dolls have a plain F.G., some F.G.s are inscribed in a scroll and some were incised F.C.G. Early, small, 8- to 9-inch dolls are charming. The larger, long-necked dolls are rare. Most F.G. dolls are a good investment. Some later dolls appear to have bloody noses because the nose paint is too low.

Françoise Gauthier was famous for his lady-doll heads. His lovely large-eye child doll heads are expensive. F.G. dolls often have low puffiness in the cheeks. They are sometimes confused with Brus, which look similar.

Gesland's stockinette-covered, padded, cork-filled body was often used with F.G. heads. A Gesland body contains a strong, jointed-metal armature. The armature allows the body to be positioned in many ways. Gesland also made composition bodies.

For many years we thought all F.G. dolls were made by *Fernand Gaultier*. Research by Florence Poisson indicates this is incorrect. Bisque heads, not dolls, were produced by *Françoise Gauthier*.

Poisson's research uncovered patent papers and inventories that indicate Gauthier used *F.G.* and *F.G. within a scroll* on bisque heads. Gauthier made porcelain doll heads for doll makers throughout France. He joined the SFBJ group in 1899.

This information also explains why we find F.G. heads on Jumeau, Gesland, Bru and other bodies.

Bisque, French, Gauthier, 28 inches, marked *10 F.G.*
She has brown paperweight eyes and a stuffed Gesland body. She is wearing her original white-lace dress.

Bisque, French, Gauthier, marked *Bébé A. Gesland, Bre S.S.D.G. 5 Ave. Beranber 5, Paris.*
Gesland's stockinette-covered, padded, cork-filled body with a strong jointed-metal armature inside allows the body to be positioned in many ways. Lower arms and legs, and the shoulder plate, are wood. The feet of this doll are interesting. Toes look like they are digging in sand.

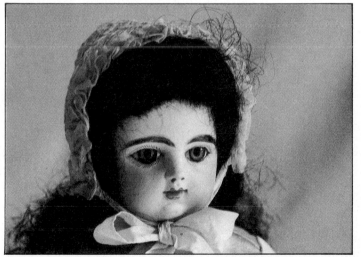

Bisque, French, Gauthier, 16 inches, marked *F.G. 3.*
The doll above has blue-lined paperweight eyes, brown kinky hair, a wood-and-composition body, original walking coat and high-heel boots.

This is the same doll at left without clothing. Lower arms and legs have an extra coat of paint to make them match the bisque head more closely. People often think these are mismatched or repainted.

Other Types of Dolls to Collect

Doll collections usually reflect the tastes and interests of the collector. A person may be interested in collecting dolls of a certain era or dolls of a particular material. Each collector must decide what theme or groups of dolls to collect.

Some people collect dolls by years. Dolls made before 1850, dolls of the 1890-1921 period and dolls of the 1920s are a few collections we have seen. Collections have been made of advertising dolls, like Morton Salt, Kelloggs, Campbell Soup, Canada Dry and other companies. Some people collect lady dolls, men dolls, child dolls or baby dolls. A collection of dolls in a series by their mold numbers, like the SFBJs, K(star)R characters, and the Simon and Halbig 900 series is not unusual.

Ethnic dolls are increasing in value. Collections of dolls by a particular doll maker are popular today, such as those by Heubach, Jumeau or Steiner. Although not considered dolls, crèche figures are often collected as dolls. Peddler dolls, made of all types of material, represent old-fashioned peddlers of household items. They can be collected. Folk dolls are collected and brought home from foreign ports, but they do not increase in value.

Most valuable collections have more than one group of dolls or more than one theme to the collection. Many collectors begin with a one-of-a-kind doll before they decide what they want to collect. Some people begin with inexpensive dolls. As their taste changes, they select

Bisque, French, Fashion doll, 14 inches.
The doll at left still wears her original costume.

Bisque, German, Simon and Halbig, marked #919.
The doll above is from the German Simon and Halbig 900 series. Her price is about the same as a French doll.

Bisque, French, Fashion dolls.
A collection of French fashion dolls is shown in a glass case that closes and locks.

Bisque, German, 7-1/2 inches, marked *I & 8/0 X*.
The girl doll has been re-dressed, but the boy doll is in his original costume. These German dolls take up little room. If you find them in original costumes, they are fun to display.

expensive dolls. People often collect over a lifetime. As their financial situation changes, so does the class of dolls they acquire.

Think about the availability of the particular dolls you want to collect. Consider how many years you have to collect dolls. You must also decide how much you can afford and the number of dolls you plan to own. Suitable exhibit space for your dolls is important. Decide whether you want a lot of dolls or a few nice ones. It takes only five dolls to make a collection.

China, German, 6 inches.
China doll with a cloth body. She wears original clothing. She has been kept under a glass dome for over 60 years.

China.
This flat-top china doll was saved as a family heirloom in its original condition. She came by covered wagon from Kentucky to Illinois. In a fire, her blouse burned off. Both of her leather hands were burned and her homespun skirt has a hole in it. She has been preserved as is. The wrapping on her chest is to hold the china shoulder head in place. No glue was available for this purpose. Her underskirt has a pocket. Skirt, underskirt and drawers are gathered by a drawstring.

China, German, 14 inches.
The black hair of this doll hangs in long curls down her back. She has a crude cloth body, with cloth stems for arms and legs. The doll has her original body and clothing, and her face paint is worn.

CHINA AND PARIAN DOLLS

China dolls have lasting characteristics and are interesting to collect. China is glazed ceramic material. These dolls are usually *shoulder heads* which is a one-piece head and shoulders.

A rare, desirable china doll has a separate head and shoulder. A china doll with glass eyes is also rare. Common china dolls sell for less than $200.

If you collect chinas for investment, look for unusual ones. These include chinas with elaborate hairstyles or bald ones that take wigs. These dolls are best for investment purposes. They may increase in value.

Some china dolls have upper arms attached to shoulders. A china head may be round, bald and glazed. Often the head has two holes through which the old wig was tied.

Parian dolls are made of white porcelain and have not been popular. Few people have been able to collect fine ones.

Parians are similar to china dolls. If you collect good ones with elaborate hairstyles, they can make a beautiful collection.

China.
Blond china doll with original clothing.

Bisque.
A bonnet bisque doll in original clothing.

China.
The dolls shown here have a variety of hairstyles. These are 5-inch and 6-inch chinas, with original costumes.

China.
This is called the *covered-wagon type* china doll because of her hairstyle.

China.
This is a blond china shoulder head. The deep shoulder plate indicates an older doll.

Parian.
This doll has a decorated shoulder plate and an original costume of silk.

Wax, English.
In her original costume, with white-flax hair, cloth body and leather boots, this peddler doll is a collector's item. She originally wore a red wool cape, but it was full of moths and moth-holes, and was discarded.

Wax, English, 17 inches.
This doll is linen-over-wax construction. She has glass eyes and a masklike face. This baby doll wears original clothing and came in her original box. She also came with a handwritten story, dated 1881. The owner of the doll died at age 4. The doll cost about 60 cents to buy when she was made.

WAX DOLLS

Peck, Pierottis, Morrell, Marsh and Montanari of England were wax-doll makers. They made their dolls with beautiful childlike heads and hands, inset hair and glass eyes. The beauty and lifelike molding and texture intrigue doll collectors.

Some wax dolls stand up well over the years. To have a lot of money invested in them could be wasteful. Any extreme temperature is not good for wax dolls.

If you have a wax doll, you may be told it needs a *wax-over* or recoating with wax. We were advised to do this with our doll. For the next year, the doll looked beautiful. Then dark gray spots started coming through the new coat of wax. We were told the gray spots were dirt that was not removed from the old wax before it was recoated. In this condition, the doll was worthless.

A friend had a split-head wax doll. This type of wax head has hair inserted in splits in the wax. The doll's head split too much the first summer she had it. It could not be repaired. She had to cover the head with a bonnet and couldn't sell the doll for what she paid for it. It was a poor investment. Be careful when purchasing a wax doll.

Wood, American, Schoenhut.
Two jointed, wooden Schoenhuts. One has molded hair and one has a wig. The girl doll has decal eyes.

Wood, American, Schoenhut.
The doll at top right is a Schoenhut girl doll.

Wood, American, Schoenhut.
Old wooden dolls from about 1912 are not often found in mint condition. They were made to be played with. Noses are usually banged up and paint is cracked off. If a doll has been repainted, its value is decreased. These wooden dolls at right are a good investment because they are American-made. They are made with complicated spring joints of solid wood.

WOODEN DOLLS

There are not many wooden dolls available for collecting. Those found are interesting and don't deteriorate or break. They are not beautiful.

Collectors interested in wooden dolls can look for the penny woodens, hand-carved woodens, Queen Anne, Schoenhuts, Joel Ellis and Mason-Taylor dolls. Penny woodens are small, jointed all-wood dolls with no fine details. Schoenhut dolls are good investments because they have complicated spring joints.

Schoenhuts, Joel Ellis and Mason-Taylor dolls were made by American doll makers. These dolls will probably increase in value in time.

The Cooperative Manufacturing Company of Joel Ellis patented wooden, jointed dolls in 1873 in Springfield, Vermont. The doll was made of wood, with the exception of cast-metal hands and lower legs with heeled shoes. Some black dolls were also produced by Ellis. The only difference was the black paint on head, shoulders, hands and legs.

Joel Ellis patents were followed by a patent for head changes by Frank D. Martin in 1879. George Sanders received patents for joint changes in 1880 and 1881. Henry Hubbard Mason and Luke Taylor patented different head and neck joints when making Mason-Taylor dolls.

Wood, American, Schoenhut.
These three dolls have painted eyes and original wigs. The blond doll has a Schoenhut dress.

Wood, American, Schoenhut, 20 inches.
Originally, a special doll-stand came with this doll. She has 2 holes in each foot. Metal pegs on the stand went into the holes in the doll's feet. If the doll wore shoes, there were holes in the shoes, too.

Wood, American, Schoenhut, 22 inches.
This spring-jointed doll has tin sleep eyes. The color of her complexion differs from older Schoenhuts.

Wood, American, Schoenhut, 20-1/2 inches.
This spring-jointed lady doll has brown eyes. Lady dolls made by Schoenhut are rare. This one has real hair tied in a knot at the back. She has long legs and arms, and a molded bosom.

Wood, American, Mason Taylor.
This doll's body is wood and its head is composition. It was made in Springfield, Vermont in the 1880s. Wooden dolls are being sought and higher prices paid for them. This is the Mason-Taylor doll sought by collectors.

Wood, American, Joel Ellis, 15 and 12 Inches, 1873.
These dolls have metal hands and feet.

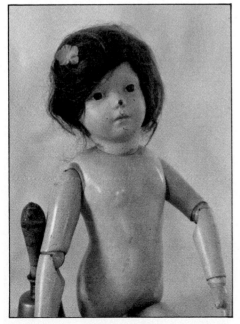

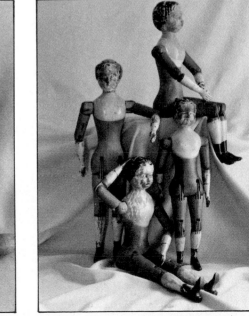

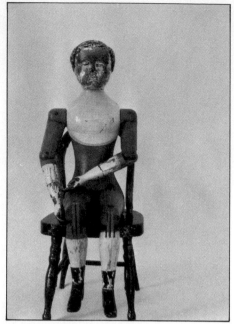

Wood, American, Joel Ellis.
The joints in this doll are intriguing. Paint did not stand up as well as the wood. Most Joel Ellis' paint looks like this. This doll costs about $200, but is difficult to find. The price of each doll depends on the part of the country it is found in and its condition.

Wood, 13 inches.
This doll has enameled eyes, a skittle-shape torso, nailed-on arms and no legs. Her enameled eyes are recessed in the wood. Her gown is silk brocade. Her excellent condition is due to the antique oval glass dome that has covered her for at least 100 years.

Wood, 15 inches.
The black irisless eyes and painted hair of this doll indicate she is old. Her worn dress is brown silk and she wears a white bonnet and collar.

Wood, English, Penny Woodens, 4 inches.
These wooden dolls are interesting.

Wood, English.
Penny Woodens were made for a long time.

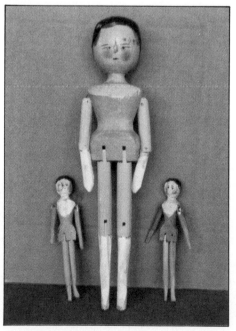

Wood, French.
This hand-carved doll has a swivel head, wooden body, arms and head, and inset glass eyes. It is a one-of-a-kind doll. Each doll was made by hand.

Bisque, French, Mechanical, 10 inches, marked *F.G.*
This doll has blue-glass eyes and is wearing its original costume. It peddles a bicycle—knees bend and the wheel turns when the doll is pushed with a rod. The doll was originally part of a large gambling wheel. It was made about 1890.

Composition, American, Mechanical, 18 inches.
The metal eyes of this mechanical carnival doll date her about 1920. She has a brass clockwork mechanism. When wound, eyes move back and forth, and the suspended grass skirt appears to dip and shake. When fully wound, the doll performs intermittently for an hour or more. This doll is valuable and fun to own.

MECHANICAL AND AUTOMATION DOLLS

Mechanical and automation dolls are engineering feats and things of beauty. These dolls move in some way. Actions are activated by an enclosed mechanism. Old French automations are desired for collections, but they require special care and housing. They are expensive to purchase. If they are in good condition, they add value to your collection. Automations or mechanicals should be in working order or partly working.

Mechanical dolls, such as the Kicking Steiner and the Walking Steiner, are usually considered better than a regular doll. If the doll works, it is worth more than an ordinary doll. If it does not work, it's not worth any more than a nonmechanical doll.

Bisque, French Automation, 13 inches, marked *G. Vichy Fils, Paris, c 1875.*
The lady has a bisque swivel head, blue-glass paperweight eyes and pierced ears. The man has a swivel head, blue-glass paperweight eyes and a cardboard torso. Both dolls are mounted on a metal base that contains a mechanism. When wound, the dolls waltz in three movements while the music box plays different tunes.

Papier-mâché.
These dolls represent one type of papier-mâché doll. They have painted eyes, molded hairstyles, wooden arms and legs, and kidiline bodies.

Papier-mâché, American, 22 inches.
The red-leather arms and legs of this doll are like many early American dolls. She has a cloth body and blue painted eyes. Hair on this doll is molded behind her ears in a gold and red snood. Formed curls in front graduate in size on the head. The gown is faded-purple print silk with a drawstring neck. She was probably made about 1850. Her face is well-modeled and has a pleasant look.

Papier-mâché, 34 inches.
The face and eyes of this doll are hand-painted. Her dress is probably original. Her white cap and white apron fell apart and had to be removed.

PAPIER-MÂCHÉ DOLLS

Papier mâché is a mixture of glue, whiting, flour, clay, and paper or wood pulp. Each doll-manufacturing company had its own mixture. Sometimes the words *papier mâché* and *composition* were used interchangeably. Usually mâché is a softer material than composition and has a cruder finish.

Some papier-mâché dolls were made a long time ago. Not many have survived. These dolls did not last in damp or wet conditions. Some are still found in fine condition, even in original costume. They have increased in value, especially glass-eye mâchés.

Milliner's Models are dolls with papier-mâché heads, leather bodies and wooden limbs. They usually had elaborate hairstyles. These dolls stand the test of time, except in certain areas where insects have eaten the mixture. They are good investments, but are not beautiful.

Milliner's Models make a fine collection. They are wonderful to study and research. With their hairstyles, they make an interesting display.

1. Composition, American, 32 inches.
The painting on this doll is unusually fine. This doll has a shoulder head, molded black hair with short curls, a cloth body, tan leather-heel boots and hands that match. She is wearing original clothing. She has painted wisps of hair on her forehead, feathered brows, fine lashes and an accented mouth. When her owner came to sell us the doll, she brought a photo of herself with the doll when she was 10 years old.

2. Composition, 11 inches.
She has a shoulder head, early blue-glass eyes, molded black boots with heels, white socks, molded arms and a sawdust-filled, commercial cloth body. Although her original silk dress is in terrible condition, her underclothing is still perfect. She has a human-hair wig.

3. Composition, American.
This is a shoulder head. She has black, molded, vertical curls, black irisless glass eyes, red-leather arms, and a cloth body and feet. She is wearing original clothing. This doll may have been repainted. Although it was a beautiful job, it decreases her value.

Composition.
A black composition doll with decal eyes. She is of unknown origin.

COMPOSITION DOLLS

Composition has been made and used for a long time. The composition of the 1880s is still good in many dolls today.

Composition can mean a variety of mixtures. It usually refers to a mixture of paper pulp, wood pulp and glue.

Dolly Dingle was a composition doll. Designed by Grace Drayton about 1910, the composition is still in good condition.

A collection of composition dolls can be divided into three time periods: before 1890, 1890 to 1920 and post-1920. Composition after 1920 is not a stable buy. It can look good one day and be full of cracks and fall apart the next day.

Horsman's composition children dolls, made from 1912 to 1915, are still intact. This is not true with all composition dolls. Be careful when buying composition dolls.

Felt, Italian, Lenci, 16 inches.
Felt dolls are interesting in a collection.

Felt, Italian, Lenci, 17 inches.
A very old puppet is shown in its original, threadbare costume.

CLOTH, RAG OR ART-FABRIC DOLLS

American cloth dolls have become popular and are increasing in value. These dirty, faded, moth-eaten dolls have a charm of their own. They are almost always found in poor condition, yet they are being collected to be preserved. Cloth dolls on uncut yardage are even more valuable. The Chase, Beecher and Emma Adams dolls have become part of many collections. They do not appeal to every collector.

Some cloth dolls were also called *printed dolls*. The form of the doll and its clothing was printed on yard goods. They were sold, taken home, cut out and sewn together. Then they were stuffed.

Felt dolls were made almost exclusively by an Italian firm, the Lenci Company. They made dolls with painted eyes. Their bright felt costumes are lovely. Like cloth, felt dolls gather grime, dampness and moth holes. They must be carefully preserved and cared for. Their prices today are too high for true value or good investment.

Metal, French, 15 inches.
A fully jointed marionette-type doll. It works by raising one or more wires. This knight was used in Opera die Pupi from the 19th century.

Bisque, German, Simon and Halbig, 6 inches.
A group of *Little Women* dollhouse dolls made to represent the characters in Louisa May Alcott's book. Some have glass eyes and some eyes are painted.

Bisque, German.
German bisque dollhouse dolls in antique or original costumes.

METAL DOLLS

There are few tin, pewter, lead, copper, aluminum and brass doll heads to be found. We had a brass boy doll with sleep eyes and no markings. Other metal heads are marked *Diana* and *Juno*. Several companies in the United States produced metal heads, but most were made in Germany. Metal doll heads do not have a lot of appeal, but are interesting.

Some dolls were made completely of metal. They were manufactured beginning in the 1860s.

DOLLHOUSE DOLLS

Dollhouse dolls are usually 1 foot to 1 inch in scale. They were made to fit inside a child's dollhouse. There were father dolls, mother dolls and child dolls. These small dolls can be displayed in many ways. Displaying them in a wall cabinet is an easy, clean way to keep many dolls.

Collecting dollhouse dolls is good for people with limited space. Contrary to what some people think, these dolls do not need a dollhouse to be displayed.

Bisque, 5 inches.
A shadowbox display of an old dollhouse doll in her original costume. She is 5 inches high.

Bisque.
This group of dollhouse dolls shows body construction. The seated lady is a glass-eye French doll of unusual beauty. Note the low shoulder plate and modeling of this doll. Dollhouse dolls make a fine collection for people with limited space and money. They do not need to be housed in a dollhouse.

Bisque, American.
Grace Corey Rockwell's *Goldie*. Note the fine modeling of the facial features and the molded hair.

Bisque.
A display of dollhouse dolls in a wall cabinet. This is an easy, clean way to keep a large number of dolls.

Leather, American.
The faces, hands and legs of the two dolls above and at right are made of glove leather. The materials for clothing were imported from France. Both dolls are perfectly weighted and balance without a doll stand. The dolls were made by Fern Deutsch. Each is an original.

Bisque, French, 10 inches, marked 106 2/0.
The doll at right is a lovely addition to a collection.

ADDITIONAL CATEGORIES FOR COLLECTING

Below is a list of other type dolls you can collect.

Dolls in original clothing
Dolls in original box
Dolls with original trunk and costumes
Molded-hair dolls
Dolls showing types of bodies
Soldier dolls
Frozen Charlottes
Cabinet-size dolls—under 16 inches
Large dolls—over 28 inches
Dolls with stories
Dolls with unusual markings
Dolls by country of origin
Motschmann-type dolls
Hand-sculptured, original dolls

Bisque, French, Jumeau, 12-1/2 inches, marked *Déposé Tête Jumeau 3 Bte S.G.D.G.*
The blue paperweight eyes, composition body marked with paper sticker, and gold mohair wig make this a good collector's doll. She is a cabinet-size doll. Her aqua-silk costume is by Pam Lembo.

Bisque, French, 8-1/2 inches, marked *4% of A, J. Steiner BSGDG Bergoin.*
These twin dolls have blue paperweight eyes, feather brows, jointed bodies and pierced ears. They are wearing original clothing.

Bisque, German, Character Boys.
These dolls have composition bodies and painted eyes. They are all under 16 inches high. Boy dolls are fun to collect. Any childlike doll is fun to collect and makes a good investment.

Celluloid, French, 15 inches, marked in relief *France 35.*
This swivel-head doll is wearing original clothing and molded shoes. She has one-piece arms and legs. Celluloid dolls are too fragile to be valuable. This one is in mint condition.

Buying Dolls

Some collectors have a feeling for dolls and prices. These people have enough foresight to buy dolls when they are priced low and watch prices rise in a short time. Recently, almost any good doll more than doubled in value in three years.

The art of buying dolls that increase in value is not difficult. More people are becoming doll collectors, but there are only the same number of old dolls. Buying a doll as an investment is not too risky. There aren't enough old dolls to go around.

A few years ago, people thought dolls were priced so high they couldn't go higher. Prices *have* gone higher. But some dolls are still reasonably priced, such as French fashion dolls, parians and china dolls. Even baby dolls can be found at fair prices.

Don't rush out and buy a large number of any type of doll, such as china dolls, hoping the price will go up. Only chinas with special hairdos or bald-headed chinas increase in value. To be valuable, a doll must have special appeal. Some baby dolls with special appeal have been good investments. These dolls will continue to go up in price.

Bisque, French, Jumeau, marked *E12 J.*
Jumeau dolls marked with E.J. are always a good investment. Note the unbroken wrists and large hands of this doll.

China, German, 20 inches.
The china doll above has a body and feet made of leather, and china hands. She is pink-tinted china with a clear glaze on the inside of her head. Shoulders and upper arms are modeled. Her head is round, bald and glazed, and has two holes through which the old wig was tied.

WHERE TO BUY DOLLS

Dolls can be purchased from doll dealers and antique shops. They can be purchased from dealers at doll shows, doll conventions and antique shows. Be careful when selecting a doll. Know the reputation of the dealer.

There are many ways to find dolls to buy. One of the best ways to purchase dolls is from another collector. Doll magazines often list dolls for sale. Shows and conventions are also an excellent source for buying from individuals.

In 1979, we ran a two-day doll clinic in New York at the Doll Artisan Guild Center. We were hoping to find some good dolls to buy. We advertised in the local paper that we would examine anyone's dolls. We would give them the approximate age, advice on repair and the value of the doll. There would be no charge for our service. We were overwhelmed with the turnout!

People came with trunks and baskets of dolls. Dolls and people overflowed the house and stood in line on the porch. People watched as we spread out a towel, undressed each doll and told its story as we went.

There were inexpensive dolls in poor condition and good dolls. Only one was for sale. Most of the dolls were family heirlooms and people wanted to know their current value. We even found a buyer for the one for sale. A man had brought it in and didn't want to take it home. We had a wonderful two days, but our hope of locating good dolls to buy for our collection vanished.

Auction companies run appraisals in cities all over the country. They find many fine dolls. As a collector, you will pay at least 30% more if you buy from an auction house rather than a private owner.

Some people are able to collect through dealers and find it satisfactory. Other people say it is too expensive. We prefer to use a combination of all the methods.

Bisque, French, Open-Mouth Jumeau.
If you have a choice between an open-mouth French doll and a closed-mouth French doll, always choose the closed-mouth one. This is true of most dolls.

Bisque, French, Schmitt.
These three Schmitt dolls have marked heads and bodies. They are all in excellent condition. The doll on the right has old clothes, but they are probably not original. Her wig was replaced. She is a good buy. The doll on the left is wearing an old pink costume, which could be original, with original wig and shoes. She is a better buy. The center doll is the best buy. She is wearing original clothing. Her clothes and hat have original labels in them. Her shoes are also marked. She has original sheepskin wig and earrings. She is in mint condition.

WHICH DOLL IS BEST?

It is good to know which are the best dolls to buy. For example, consider three Jumeau dolls. One has a few red marks, one a stamped Tête Jumeau on the neck and the third has an incised Déposé Jumeau. They would be rated good, better and best buy in that order.

Three similar Jumeaus might be more difficult to rate. One has no clothes, one has reproduction clothes and the other has her old costume. A Jumeau with no clothes is a good buy. The one with reproduction clothes is a better buy. The one with an old costume in good condition is the best buy.

Suppose three dolls are almost the same, but one has a hairline crack, one has a chipped ear and the third has a worn body. The doll with a hairline would be a poor buy, the one with an ear chip a good buy and the worn body an excellent buy.

If you acquire a Bru, it is fun to have two Brus. If you get the K(star)R 114 you wanted, try for a brown-eyed one, one with glass eyes, a bigger one, a smaller one or one in original clothes. Doll collecting should be a continuing thing. It should never lose its excitement.

When the doll you want comes along with a broken finger or a less-than-perfect body, buy it. If the same type of doll comes along again and is perfect, buy that one and sell the first.

ACQUIRING DOLLS

Have an ever-changing list of dolls you would like to acquire. When one doll is acquired, add another doll to the list. Send your list to several doll dealers. Sometimes a dealer will call you on a particular doll before he advertises it. You are at the dealer's mercy regarding the price. If a dealer locates a certain doll, notifies you and you don't take the doll, he won't call again.

Never hesitate to drive a few miles or make a few long-distance telephone calls to find a doll. You never know what you'll find. Our little No. 3 A.T. came from an estate in Leadville, Colorado. The doll had been newly acquired by a doll maker who saw a resemblance to one of our reproduction A.T.s. She called us for help identifying the doll. After several telephone calls, we offered a high price for the doll, then increased it. After a few weeks, the doll maker decided to sell us the doll. It has made a fine addition to our French collection. It is an excellent example of an A.T. on an original leather body in superb condition. It is one of our favorite dolls.

Sometimes these experiences are not happy. Over the telephone, a dealer offered us a large No. 14 A.T. that we wanted. We had limited time and drove to Indianapolis from New York without stopping. The doll was a disappointment because it was poor quality and open-mouth. We decided to buy it anyway. We used the doll for a mold, then sold it.

We found our Marque dolls by chance. we saw the two dolls in a collection. We made the collector an offer, which she refused. Three years later, we called her again. She said a dealer had offered her $12,000 each for the dolls, but she still was not interested in selling them. When we offered her the right price for one doll, she agreed to sell it, if we picked it up. It was a 4-day trip, but we made the trip and bought the doll. The following year, when we called again, she agreed to sell the other doll for the same price. We had to make the four-day trip again.

These dolls took care of our doll-buying budget for awhile. But we have never regretted the investment we made in these two perfect dolls in original costumes. We bought the dolls when they were available. We might never have had the opportunity again.

Bisque, French, Marque.
One of the Albert Marque dolls we traveled four days for.

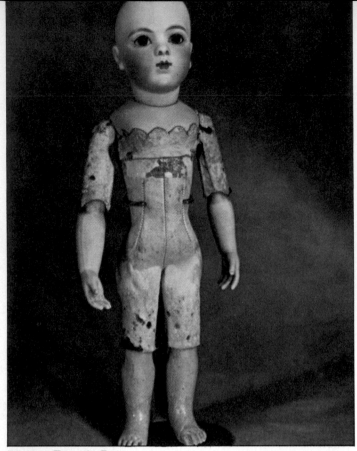

Bisque, French, Bru.
Check the doll carefully if you are buying an investment doll, such as this Bru.

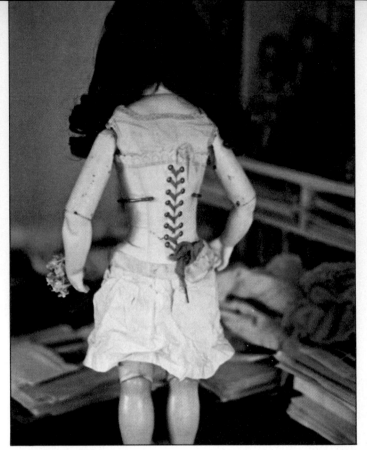

Undress the doll.

STEPS IN BUYING A DOLL

There are a few steps to follow when buying a bisque doll. These steps can save you time, money and unhappiness. It may seem like a lot of work, but if you are buying an investment doll and paying between $1,000 and $10,000, it is best to know what is under the wig and clothing.

Study the doll. Decide if you like her and need her. Look up the doll in as many books as possible. Check photos and markings. Find out all you can about the doll. When you inspect the doll, check markings to see if they are what you expected. Do this *yourself*.

With a magnifying glass, check the bisque. Look for chips or repairs around the eyes, hairline cracks, chips from ear lobes and cracks in the base of the neck or rim of the head. Remove the wig and pate to look inside.

A strong light or a black light helps locate cracks and repairs. The light must be shown through the bisque head. If you use a black light in a dark room, all the cracks and repairs show. We once bought a Jumeau. When we tried out our black light on her, we found numerous cracks that had been repaired.

Look for stains on the bisque. If they are removable, the seller would have removed them. Check bisque for smoothness, color and paint. There should be no color rubbed off the flesh-color face, showing white marks.

Study the eyes. Decide what kind of eyes the doll was supposed to have. If they are paperweight eyes, be sure they match and have not been replaced. If they are sleep eyes, they should sleep. Even Googlies with glass eyes should sleep.

Most doll collectors prefer original wigs. Study the wig to see if it has possibilities. Is it mohair, human hair or a synthetic wig?

Ask to see the doll with her clothing off. Perhaps the body is unusual, has been replaced or mismatched parts have been added. Expect wear on leather or composition bodies, because dolls were probably played with.

While the doll is undressed, check proportions to see if they are pleasing. Don't buy a big head on a small body or a small head on a big body.

Sometimes you may buy undressed dolls, but it is better to buy dolls in costumes. There is no substitute for an original costume. A doll in original clothing is more valuable. Old shoes are highly desirable. It is almost impossible to locate old shoes to fit. New shoes are not the same. If the doll is undressed, you should pay less for it.

If a doll is dressed, try not to be influenced by a bonnet or pretty dress. Judge the doll from the inside out.

If you follow these steps, you will usually know what you have bought. It is almost impossible to find perfect dolls, so don't become obsessed with perfection.

Often, you don't have time to go through these steps. We have purchased dolls from owners by simply asking if there are any cracks or repairs. We usually believe doll people. Some of our loveliest dolls were purchased without our touching them.

An auction is different. At auctions, find out what you are bidding on. Always allow yourself enough viewing time. Ask questions and ask to look at the dolls you are interested in.

Most reputable dealers are dependable enough to buy through the mail, usually with a three-day return privilege. Take advantage of this service if a dealer has a doll you are interested in purchasing.

AUCTION BUYING

Buying dolls at auctions can be fun and a learning experience at the same time. We have attended all kinds of auctions, not just doll auctions. We have had many experiences at doll auctions, both good and bad.

The following story illustrates two important points about auctions. First, auctions allow a doll collector to find dolls that might never be found any other way. Second, if you research the dolls you are interested in, you may be able to buy an excellent doll that other collectors do not realize is valuable.

We fell in love with two dolls we saw in a book. We never thought they would be sold at auction. In 1981, a Huret child doll and a pair of French automated dancers came up for sale at auction.

The unusual French automated dancers was a lovely waltzing pair with a music box underneath. They were from the collection of Fanchon Canfield. We bid $5,200 and got them.

The other doll was a beautiful Mason Huret with a wooden, jointed body. It was undressed, but had its old, slightly threadbare costume with it. The head of this doll did not fit down into the wooden body as far as most bisque heads go into composition bodies. Some viewers thought there was something wrong with it. Research had turned up photographs of at least two similar dolls. We were sure it was acceptable. We con-

We bought this doll without even removing her from her glass cabinet. The dealer who had her was reliable. We believed her when she said there were no cracks.

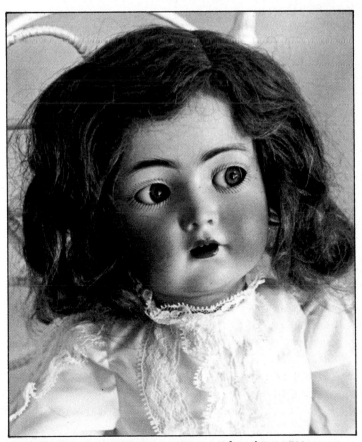

Bisque, German, 20 inches, marked *K (star)R 117N.*
This doll has blue eyes that sleep. She was re-dressed by her original owner.

sidered the doll a rare find and bought it for $8,300. We have been pleased with these dolls we bought at this auction.

Each auction is different. Sometimes there are no dolls worth bidding on. At other times, there will be an auction where you want to make many bids. It's hard to decide which dolls to bid on. Don't bid on dolls you don't want because they're selling for a low price. Save your money and buy one good doll.

Sometimes you can take advantage of the type of auction or the type of collector attending the auction. At one auction, where collectors came to buy special high-priced dolls, many excellent baby dolls and German dolls sold for low prices. This was the time to buy them.

Attending an auction provides the chance to study the catalog and the dolls. You can see the dolls, their markings, repairs and different costumes. An auction gives you an opportunity to decide what kind of dolls you like and want. Your catalog is a good reference tool.

When you go to an auction, carefully study the dolls. The light is usually poor, so take a lighted magnifier if possible. You may ask questions of the auction attendant. You should ask to see anything not fully described or anything you have a question about.

Use information you gain through research to evaluate each doll. Imagine it with a different costume or another wig. If a doll has original wig and costumes, they should not be changed. If they are not original, a costume of your choice may be better.

As a beginning collector, you should attend a few doll auctions to learn how they work and what types of dolls are sold. Study the catalog before you go. Leave your money at home. Your first few auctions are to study dolls and the auction system. Different auction houses operate differently.

Preparing To Buy At Auction—When you think you have a feeling for how auctions work, it's time to buy a doll at auction. Order the catalog early. Study it before you go.

Catalog study is important. You can learn a lot about many kinds of dolls by reading doll descriptions and studying photos. Go through the catalog quickly to see if there is anything you must have. Then go through the catalog carefully. Read *every* description. Mark in the catalog all breaks, chips, hairlines, unmatched bodies and other faults. This calls your attention to these as bidding proceeds.

Bisque, French, Jumeau.
An unmarked Jumeau and E.J. Note open mouths and paperweight eyes.

When reading catalog descriptions, try to determine if the body is the correct one. Your past study of dolls may help here, or you may have to do additional research on the dolls. Be aware of *hairline cracks*, which are small cracks and *color rubs*, which are places where color has worn off. These are bad or they would not be mentioned. If the catalog does not say the costume is old or original and in excellent condition, it is probably worthless.

If the catalog states hands or body are worn, they are probably very worn. If the photo is not from the front and full-length, try to figure out why.

Select a few dolls you're interested in. Research these dolls for historical background. Look up markings and numbers. Study price guides and old auction books. If the dolls you wish to bid on are unfamiliar to you, look them up in as many places as possible.

Bisque, French, Jumeau, 28 inches.
Open-mouth French dolls are good to collect. They do not have the same value as closed-mouth French dolls. This 28-inch Tête Jumeau sits in a chair.

China.
An old china doll with color rubs on her face. Color rubs are places where the cheek color is completely worn through to the white porcelain underneath, usually caused by years of rough play by children.

Try to establish a value for each doll you want. Any values you find may be from the previous year's price guide or auction, so the current price will probably be higher. If possible, try to find out previous selling prices for similar dolls.

Make a list of the dolls, with the highest prices you will offer and total it. Cross off the list until you have a figure you can afford. Read the condition of the dolls again. Usually only the worst things are mentioned. Many are missed!

Mark your catalog in code. Using this code, write what you will pay for the doll in the catalog. Don't mark your catalog in any obvious way, because someone may look over your shoulder. Don't discuss your intentions with anyone but your family.

Buying At Auction—If the auction is held more than 100 miles away, make reservations at a hotel near where it will be held. Go the day before so you have time to preview the dolls.

Take only enough money with you to buy the dolls you select. Before you leave, put several boxes and packing materials in your car. This is to carry home any dolls you buy.

Be at the auction room when it opens. Wear comfortable clothing and shoes. Take a camera, a lighted magnifier and a clipboard for notes.

Look at the dolls with the catalog and light magnifier in hand. Make a note of any dolls you like and may want to bid on. Go back and carefully study the dolls on your list. If one doesn't look good, cross it off.

Ask an attendant to take down any dolls you're interested in. Check repairs, paint, wig, clothing and other details. If there are two dolls from the same maker and a variation of the same mold, auction catalogers usually offer the poorer doll first. This seems to raise total bids.

Before the auction starts, go back over your list of dolls and top bids. Check in at the auction table for a customer number and to establish your credit. The auction house needs to know how you are going to pay your bill.

When the dolls are being sold, pay attention to the proceedings. Bid on any dolls you want to buy. If someone bids a higher price than you are willing to pay for a doll, stick with your original price.

At some auctions, there are absentee bids. Absentee bids are sent in by people who cannot attend the auction. If there is more than one absentee bid, that's the place the bidding starts. Sometimes more than half the dolls go to absentee bidders. An auction clerk bids for absentee bidders.

Doll dealers from various places across the country may be scattered around the hall. They bid on many dolls, hoping to buy them at a low price and sell them for a higher price in their shops.

Usually the last 15 dolls at an auction are not high quality. The audience begins to sift out when the last doll they are interested in has been sold.

After the auction, you must pay the bill for any dolls you buy. Check each price carefully, then pick up the dolls. This is a critical time, so you *must* know what the catalog states. Examine purchases carefully. You have a chance to pick up the doll and look at it closely. This is your last chance to check the doll. If you sign the papers, it indicates you accept the doll.

After you buy your dolls, you must get them home safely. The auction does not supply boxes and packing materials. The materials you brought with you are used for this purpose. Pack your purchases carefully. When you get home with your dolls and start to undress them to clean them, you may still be in for some surprises.

Auction Rules—There are certain rules to follow when buying a doll at an auction. Read and study these rules *before* you buy at an auction. Follow them as closely as you can.

1. Study and select dolls carefully before the auction.
2. Make decisions on spending limits and on dolls.
3. Select substitute dolls.
4. Enter the auction hall with confidence. Even if you intend to bid the smallest amount on the poorest doll, you are important. The auction cannot run without bidders.
5. If you missed something on a doll, ask to see it. Don't be intimidated by the auctioneer or other buyers. You are important. But don't waste the time of the auctioneer with unnecessary questions or looking.
6. Be attentive. Don't let dolls pass while you are not paying attention.
7. When the doll you want comes along, be confident. Hold your hand up high so the auctioneer can see it. Leave it there until the auctioneer reaches your top limit.
8. Another way to bid is to see where a doll's price is going. Get in on the second going, when the auctioneer says "Going, going . . ." before he says "Gone!"
9. Don't visit with or distract people near you.
10. Don't go in and out of the hall more than necessary.
11. Never ask your friends not to bid on a doll because you want it.
12. Upon examination of a doll after auction, don't hesitate to reject a misrepresented doll. Any major faults must be in the catalog.

Auction Terms—Below are some abbreviations you will find in auction catalogs and advertisements. Study them so you will know what they mean.

4 UP	4 upper teeth
JCB	Jointed, composition body
HH	Human-hair wig
M	Mohair wig
OM	Open mouth
P eyes	Painted eyes
PW eyes	Paperweight eyes
Ptd.	Painted (usually repainted)
Rep.	Repaired
S. eyes	Sleep eyes
SH	Shoulder head

OM is used for an open mouth in advertisements. This doll has an open mouth, *4UP*, 4 upper teeth, and *S eyes*, sleep eyes, set to the side.

List Of Auctions—Below is a list of auctions held around the country. Check to see if any are held in your area.

- *Richard W. Withington, Inc.*
  Hillsboro, NH 03244 (603) 464-3232
  Holds cataloged auctions about once a month. There is no absentee bidding.
  Black-and-white catalog—$7.00.
- *Auctions by Theriaults*
  P.O. Box 151, Annapolis, MD 21404 (301) 269-0681
  Holds auctions about once a month. Has cataloged and uncataloged auctions in and around major cities. Moves from place to place. Allows absentee bidding.
  Color catalog—$15.00.
- *Kenneth S. Hays & Associates, Inc.*
  4740 Bardstown Rd., Louisville, KY 40218 (502) 499-8942
  Holds doll auctions when he has a collection to sell. Watch doll magazines for times and places.

Other auction houses that sell dolls periodically:

- *Richard A. Bourne Co., Inc.*
  P.O. Box 141, Hyannis Port, MA 02647
- *Christies*
  012 E. 67th St., New York, NY 10021
- *Dumouchelle Art Galleries Co.*
  409 E. Jefferson Ave., Detroit, MI 48226
- *Sotheby Park Bernet*
  1334 York Ave. at 72nd St., New York, NY 10021
- *Sotheby Park Bernet*
  7660 Beverly Blvd., Los Angeles, CA 90036

Absentee Bidding—Buying dolls by absentee bid from an auction is a common practice. But it has problems. If you haven't examined the doll, you buy it sight unseen. It's difficult to read what is not written in a catalog description.

We have participated in absentee bidding in several auctions. At two auctions, we didn't get any of the dolls. We bid what we believed was $200 to $300 over the current value. At another auction, we bid higher than value and got a Schmitt doll in excellent condition. We weren't unhappy, except we didn't like the replacement wig and costume.

The doll at left was acquired by absentee bid from an auction. She is shown as she came from the auction.

The same doll is shown at right. She is undressed to show body size, which was incorrect. She is 19 inches high.

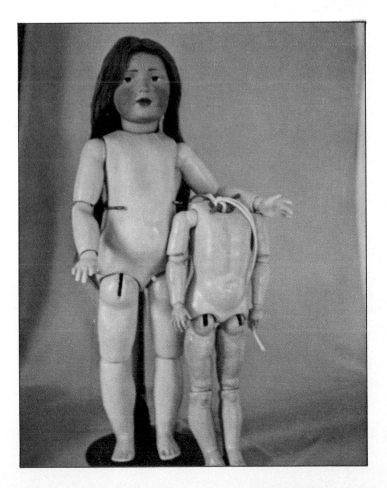

This is the same doll again. Now she is on the correct-size body and wears an old replacement wig. Beside her is the body she originally came on. Her correct body size is 27 inches.

Advertisements state you pay only what competing bids go up to. We took a chance on two dolls, bid a high price and paid a lot of money. The dolls, even though rated as top dolls, were not high quality. The catalog did not show the bodies. One had the wrong body, some repair and a replaced wig. The other doll had a body that was too small. Neither was worth the price we paid.

The first doll had rubs through the cheek color that were not mentioned in the written description. We asked the auctioneers to take it back and they did. They gave us credit for the value of the doll for a future auction, but the cost of shipping both ways was lost.

The second, a K(star)R 109, had been described in the catalog as having a unique body. It was unique—the body was four sizes too small for the head. She was freshly strung, as though the head had been found and put on an available body.

We kept this doll because we wanted a large K(star)R 109. We had the correct body. Now with the doll dressed as it was originally, with an antique wig, will her value increase? We paid so much it won't, but we're happy to have a doll we wanted for so long.

At one auction, we sent an absentee bid on two dolls and got one, a Bru. Her photo was not attractive, but we were familiar with the number and marking. If she had no cracks or repair, we felt we were safe. We were pleased with the doll. It was a high price to pay, but we haven't seen that same type of doll for sale since we started collecting.

At another auction we sent an absentee bid for two dolls. We got neither doll.

There are several ways to look at absentee bidding. It is a chancy, expensive way to buy dolls. But you might get a doll you have not seen for sale anywhere else. We have bid high and low, bid on different types of dolls, and returned dolls. It has all been an interesting experience.

OTHER WAYS TO PURCHASE DOLLS

As a collector, you will want to find other sources to buy dolls. Listed below are other places you may find dolls for sale.

Dolls From Owners—An excellent way to buy a doll is from its original owner. Dolls that have been moved from place to place, exhibited, handled, re-dressed and re-wigged are not always the best buy. Dolls sold at auction may have had rough treatment.

The doll from page 125 is cleaned and dressed in a costume similar to those of other dolls of this type. Her moth-eaten wig has been changed to an antique, long-hair wig.

The value of this doll is not known, but dressed in a proper wig and on the correct-size body, she is more attractive and pleasing to own.

Look for original owners of dolls for the best price and value. These dolls have often been stored in trunks or drawers for years. Try to find the woman who was a childhood tomboy and didn't play with dolls. You may find a doll in superior condition.

When dealing with someone who is not knowledgable about prices, pay the true value of the doll. Don't be greedy. If you pay too little, your reputation soon catches up with you.

Dolls In Your Mailbox—More dolls are purchased by mail than any other way. It is not a bad way to buy a doll. Mail-order dolls usually come from dealers who place advertisements in papers and magazines, or from private individuals selling one or two dolls. Even absentee-auction bid dolls must come through the mail.

Valuable dolls cannot be shipped by UPS or other conventional methods. Insurance does not cover antiques. Shipping through the Post Office by registered, insured mail is the best way. It is sometimes quicker and less expensive.

Dolls purchased through the mail often have a three-day return privilege. This is usually enough time for you to decide whether you will keep the doll or not. Be sure to deal with reputable people. You might get caught with a dealer holding a check on a returned doll.

Buying Dolls Abroad—Buying dolls in Europe is the same as it is in this country. They have high prices and broken dolls, too. Dealers with contacts in Europe, who buy periodically, do well. To take a trip to buy dolls is difficult now that Europeans are collecting as ardently as we are. If you add the cost of the trip to the price of the doll, it's not worth it. But if you are going anyway, there is the fun of hunting.

DOLL CHEATS

Doll cheats are found almost anywhere dolls are sold. Cheats can include dealers, other collectors, an individual seller at a doll convention and auction catalogers. This is not a problem if you are cautious and examine a doll thoroughly before you buy.

Doll cheats are people who disguise, paint over or cover up a defect that would decrease the price of a doll. Some of the most common defects to look for are wrong-size bodies or substituted, unmatched parts, head cracks or chips where hair has been firmly glued down to cover it, glued-in-place sleep eyes, major repairs to bisque that have been painted over, and repairs

to bisque around eyes, later touched up with paint. Ear chips are common where earrings have been put in, but this is not a major fault.

A black light in a dark room, shown through a bisque head, shows cracks and repairs. If the doll is expensive, take time to undress it and look inside its head before purchasing. There is a doll hospital in New York that coats the inside of the head with a material after repairs are done so light doesn't show through. We know this from experience. We bought a large Jumeau that was repaired and coated there. After making a mold of the head, we could detect repairs.

CREATING A MARKET

The doll market is sometimes manipulated by doll-auction companies. This is done by communication through doll magazines, color folders, television and other media. If an auction sells a Bru for $16,500, they advertise this hoping a Bru at the next auction will be bid up to that price. Suddenly, everyone who owns a Bru feels their doll is worth $16,500. They forget about the crack in the head and its new costume.

All articles concerning high prices build up the market. Sometimes dolls of little value can be sold for high prices simply by advertising, talking about it in seminars and improving its appearance by an unusual photographic angle.

Bisque, German, Googly, 16 inches, marked *K(star)R, Simon & Halbig 131.*
Monday wears original clothing and hair. The doll above was purchased through the mail after a telephone call.

Caring for the Collection

Much of the fun of having a doll collection is sharing it. You can share the joy of collecting with your spouse. You can share your collection with your children, relatives and friends, as well as your doll club. It may be possible to share your dolls with the people in your area. Dolls were made for the pleasure of children, but they can be enjoyed by many people.

You can share your dolls without opening your doors. Doll pictures can appear in books or magazines where many people will see them. They can also appear in local newspapers. You can show them on television. Some dolls can be displayed in closed, locked cases at libraries, museums and schools. Some department stores like to hold displays and exhibits.

There are places where it is possible to show less-valuable dolls. Showing your treasures may inspire others to collect or become interested in dolls.

Some collectors are overly concerned with the security of their dolls. The fear of theft or financial loss causes them to lose the joy their dolls should give them. Your doll collection should not be a chore. Don't exhibit your dolls or make speeches if you don't want to. Be in charge of your collection.

Churches, banquets, school classes and clubs are always looking for speakers if you enjoy giving programs. Use discretion in selecting dolls you transport and show. Less-breakable dolls do as well and can make just as interesting a talk. If you are a member of the United Federation of Doll Clubs, you can exhibit dolls at shows or at regional and national conventions.

Bisque, German, Kestner.
An almost-perfect *Hilda,* by Kestner, is shown at left.

Wood, American, Joel Ellis.
Dolls can be exhibited at doll shows, fairs and conventions. The wooden Joel Ellis doll shown above will probably wear her ribbon forever.

Taking slides and showing them with a talk is a good way to exhibit your dolls with little or no risk. This method of sharing keeps your dolls secure. There is no breakage and more people can see your dolls. Slides can be sent around the country to show friends or groups. It is a safe, fun way to share your dolls.

DOLL RECORD

Keep a record of your doll collection. Some people keep long, complicated records of each doll bought or sold, while others keep no records at all. A middle course is best. Always have photographs as part of any record. For owners of large collections, keeping records can be a burden. It may take the joy out of collecting. Our theory is to enjoy the dolls and keep records as simple as possible.

Collectors need to work out a system that is easy for them. File cards, a notebook or cards printed for this purpose work well.

Include the following data for each doll.

1. Doll's name, if it is important to you.
2. Material of the head, such as bisque, composition, wax.
3. Size.
4. Type of doll, such as lady, child, baby, boy.
5. Markings. Use all numbers, initials and symbols.
6. Maker, such as Kestner, Jumeau, Bru or others.
7. Country of origin, such as Germany, France, United States.
8. Price paid and date.
9. Where purchased.
10. Any price changes of the doll.
11. Description of costume, complete with underclothing.
12. Description of flaws, replaced parts or repairs to the doll.

If you prefer a short record, the following are the most important things to include: size, material of head, name of doll, markings, price paid and up-to-date price. Have a picture with this description. This information will help if you want a friend or relative to inherit all or part of your collection. It's not a difficult record to keep.

Some people don't like to record data because other people can find out how much they paid for a doll. Devise a code. One code is *Black Horse*, where letters are changed to numbers. One through ten, from right to left, gives the price paid for an item. For example, an item costing $4,725 would read OCSH. Any word or words of 10 different letters can be used.

Some collectors put information on a tag on the doll and pin it under her clothing. It is probably best to have it in a notebook *and* on the doll. If the doll has an unusual history or story connected with it, record it and keep it with the doll.

PRESERVING THE DOLL

Caring for and preserving dolls is an important part of any doll collection. You must be prepared to spend time keeping your dolls in the best condition possible.

Preserve Old Costumes—The costume of one doll or a collection of dolls is important. A new collector may want to immediately strip the doll and throw old clothing in the garbage. This is like throwing away a piece of the doll or a bit of its history.

Sometimes an old costume can be cleaned, sometimes it cannot. If you feel the costume is completely gone, have it copied in material as much like the original as possible.

If there is no costume, as is often the case with auction dolls, use the library or your own reference books to see what costumes the doll or similar dolls wore. Sometimes reprints of old

Bisque, French, Gauthier, 11 inches, marked *F.G.3*.
This beautiful doll has blue-lined eyes, a blond mohair wig and a jointed, composition body. This doll lost her original clothing because her owner felt the costume was too old!

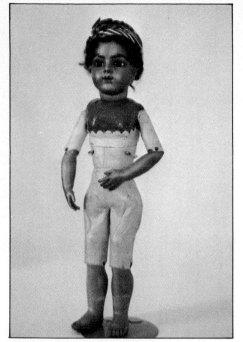

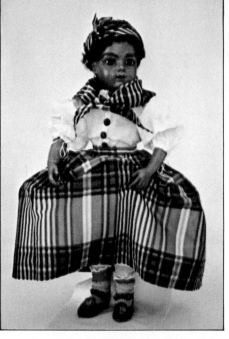

Bisque, French, Bru, marked *Bru Jne 7.*
This beautiful doll came to us from the owner and is in mint condition. *Daliah* has a black-mohair wig, brown-black paperweight eyes, bisque arms, wooden legs and a leather body. She wears her original dress, underclothing, shoes and socks.

Bisque, French, 11-1/2 inches, marked *Jullien 1.*
This doll has blue paperweight eyes, her original chemise and human hair. She is prize in her old costume.

catalogs of dolls are a good source for original costumes.

Patterns for doll costumes are available from doll makers. Many patterns have been made directly from old costumes. Fine laces and antique ribbons may be purchased from French wig importers. There are a few people who make handmade shoes similar to old ones. Choosing the right color, material and trims for costumes for a collection of undressed dolls is part of collecting and maintaining a fine collection.

Some collectors carefully remove all wool garments. Many dolls come with wool petticoats, socks, diapers, sweaters or other garments. Removing these is a precaution against moths or museum pests. It may be wise to do this, but you must decide for yourself.

To get rid of or prevent museum pests or moths, add a one-inch strip of *Shell No-Pest Strip* to doll cabinets. Hang the piece so it does not touch anything or set it in a small, open box. It might discolor something if it touches it. Strips may gather moisture on the surface.

Wigs—Wigs on French and German dolls were made from Tibetan goat or human hair. Many original wigs were cut by the child owner,

became moth-eaten or were combed until there was little hair left. A doll with an original wig is more valuable than a doll with a replacement wig. If the doll's charm and beauty are lost because her wig is no longer attractive, replace the wig with another old one or a new human-hair wig. With care, some wigs can be washed and restyled.

Human hair washes better than mohair. Old sheepskin wigs cannot be washed, so handle them carefully.

Do as little as possible to old costumes, wigs and shoes. Don't paint bodies, change eyes or throw away cork pates. Keep the doll as original as possible.

Cleaning A Doll—We always wash our dolls' faces because we like clean faces and shining eyes. We clean bisque dolls with *409* cleaner. We use a cotton tip to clean ears and noses. We wipe the body with *Johnson's Jubilee* liquid kitchen wax. This takes away the musty odor and cleans off surface grime without injuring water-soluble painted composition. *Never* wash a composition body because paint will wash off.

Replacing Parts—If you have dolls with missing parts, their value will not change much by adding replacement parts. It is only in rare in-

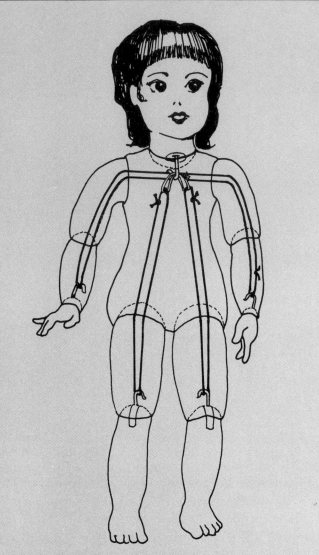

RESTRINGING BISQUE DOLLS

Step 1 GET READY
Cut old elastic in both knee joints and remove. Carefully pull head. Secure head hook so you won't lose it.

Step 2 ARMS
Cut old arm elastic and remove. Measure new elastic from the wrist across the chest to the other wrist. Double this measurement. Thread doubled elastic through the upper and lower arm. Loop elastic over hand hook. Pull tight and attach clamp on elastic at shoulder. String both ends of elastic through body, down through other upper arm, then through lower arm. Unclamp shoulder and pull elastic tight. Clamp elastic at the wrist. Tie ends of elastic in a knot or sew together with thread. Loop elastic over hand-hook and unclamp. Release carefully.

Step 3 LEGS
Measure new elastic for legs from knee to neck. Double this measurement. Add 4 inches on large dolls to make tying easier. Thread elastic down through upper legs. Hook lower legs. Use stringing hook to hook elastic at the neck of body. Pull tight and clamp. Tie elastic for each leg together. Tie another short elastic from one leg loop to the other. Pull this single loop up and clamp enough so you can hook the head into it. Unclamp head and ease into socket.

stances you can find an antique part to match exactly. Study a reproduction-parts catalog to find the same type of body and the nearest size possible to your doll. We prefer to replace both legs or both hands if one is missing. A doll is lovelier to look at when she is complete.

At auction, you may purchase a doll, then find it is on the wrong-size body. You can change the body. We could never figure out why we didn't like a Jumeau we had. When we opened the stitched-on jacket, we found the head did not fit. The body was too small. We are still looking for a large, antique-Jumeau body. We may have to change her to a reproduction body.

Restringing Bisque Dolls—Many dolls must be *restrung*. Restringing means to put in new elastic. You can learn to do this yourself. It is less expensive and safer. But it does not increase or decrease the value of the doll.

A doll that needs to be restrung may have her legs hanging, her head hanging to one side or hands dangling. Old dolls were strung in various ways. Study how it was done in your doll by looking at how it was strung when you take her apart. Also look at the illustration on this page.

Use a table with a couple of layers of bath towels as an operating table. Have plenty of room, adequate time and a helper if the doll is large.

You will need round doll-elastic, appropriate for the size of the doll. This can be purchased from any doll-supply house. You will also need a stringing hook—commercial or made from hanger wire—a pair of pliers and a hemostat or clamp.

Dolls vary in the way they were originally strung. It is difficult to say whether the wig will have to be removed for restringing or not. You will soon be able to tell.

Lay the doll on the table and make sure her head won't roll off. Cut the old elastic in the knee joint. Be careful that the hook in the lower leg does not snap back inside the leg. Cut *both* leg elastics. This usually loosens the head, but not always. Carefully pull up on the head. Attach something to the head hook so you will not lose it up in the head. If you lose the hook in the head, take off the doll's wig and pate to retrieve it.

Next, cut the arm elastic. Measure the new elastic from the wrist across the chest to the other wrist. Double this measurement. You won't waste elastic this way.

Thread the doubled elastic down through the upper arm and lower arm. Hook the hand hook over the loop in the elastic. Pull tight. Attach a clamp on the elastic at the shoulder.

String both ends of elastic through the body, down through the other upper arm, then through the lower arm. Unclamp the shoulder and pull the elastic tight. Clamp elastic at the wrist. Tie the two ends of the elastic in a knot or bind them together with thread. Hook the hand hook into the elastic loop and unclamp. Release it carefully.

Start the legs by measuring from the knee to the neck and double this measurement. Add about 4 inches on large dolls to make tying easier. Do this for both legs. Thread the elastic down through the upper legs. Hook on the lower legs.

Using the stringing hook, pull leg elastic up through the neck. Pull the elastic tight and clamp it. Tie the elastic for each leg together as tight as possible. Tie another short elastic from one leg loop to the other. Pull this single loop up enough so you can hook the head into it. Have someone hold the head. Unclamp it and ease the head into the socket. The doll should be stiff.

Baby dolls with curved limbs can be strung in several ways. A good way is to hook the arm hook into a loop of elastic. Double elastic is then strung through one armhole to the other. The other arm hook is hooked into the elastic. Elastic is pulled snug on the opposite side and held by the clamp and tied.

To attach legs, thread a double piece of elastic down through the neck hole. Hook it on both legs. Pull the elastic snug at the neck, clamp it and tie it in a knot. If the legs pull up on the body, you may have the elastic too tight.

Hook the head into the loop and unclamp the elastic. On some dolls, the elastic needs to be held together above the navel. This can be done with string or wire through a leg hole.

Repairing Bodies—Early Bru bodies are made of leather, including legs and feet. These bodies often become bent or distorted, so they neither sit nor stand. It is impossible to put the doll on a stand or to sit it in a chair.

We decided to do something about this. The upper part of the body of the doll was stuffed with ground cork. The joint area was filled with wool. Legs and feet were stuffed with sawdust. Inside, a flexible metal rod went down through the body and legs.

We took the most warped, deformed Bru body

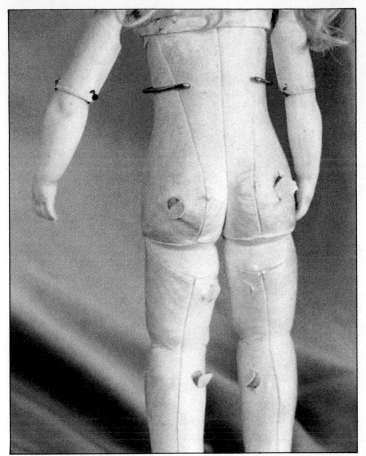
This shows where we operated on our Bru body. We removed enough filler to straighten her body.

we had and operated on it. At first we were going to open a seam. Doll seams are hard to resew, so we decided against it. We took a scalpel and cut a round hole in each hip, upper leg, calf and foot. We saved the circle we removed. We made the cuts on the back and inside, where it would show the least.

After removing some cork and wool from the hips, we worked the cork in the doll body. We did the same with the upper leg until the joint area was flexible enough to bend back into shape. Next, we removed some sawdust and worked the lower legs and feet until they turned to a normal position. The metal rod in the doll was also bent back.

We dampened the leather on the heavily wrinkled area on the front of the legs. We put the doll face-down, with a towel under its face. We weighted the body with books and let the leather dry overnight.

The next day, when we removed the books and looked at the doll, we were amazed! It was hard to believe the deformed body could look so

Our Jumeau is preserved in a 36-inch antique glass dome.

The wall cabinet shows how small dolls can be stored safely, while still being visible.

good. To patch the holes, we put a larger circle of leather inside each hole. We applied rubber cement to both pieces and replaced the circle of leather we had cut out.

HOUSING THE DOLL COLLECTION

Antique dolls are works of art and pieces of history. A doll collection should be treated and displayed as an art collection. An owner should be able to see and enjoy the dolls.

The setting for dolls sometimes gives them a new dimension. These toys become sculptures. They create interest if displayed properly. Fine doll cabinets with lights and glass can be purchased to match furniture. Doll cabinets can be built into walls and covered with glass doors. Shelves in the cabinets can be adjusted to the size of the dolls.

Keep your doll cabinets locked. Some people have alarms inside their cabinets. Dolls should always be insured. Keep accurate records on purchase price and dates. Photographs of each doll or a collection of dolls should be kept with other records in a safe-deposit box.

Dolls under glass domes are well-protected and beautiful. Large domes are usually antiques and not easily found. Smaller domes are sold on

A glass-and-brass cabinet holds tiny dolls.

A display cabinet shows one way to house dolls. The cabinet locks and has sliding glass doors to keep dolls safe.

the market. There are other glass cases with brass edges for tiny dolls. Some dolls can be placed around the house on display.

If you must store a doll, wrap it carefully before putting it away. Sleep-eye dolls should be stored face down to protect the eye mechanism. Wrap dolls in cotton towels for storage.

MOLDS FROM DOLLS

Doll collectors, especially those with fine dolls, are often approached by doll-mold makers. Mold makers want to borrow dolls to make molds for reproduction dolls. Sometimes collectors volunteer their dolls.

I have been involved in the doll-mold business and have made hundreds of molds from antique dolls. *Never let your doll be used for a mold.* A doll from which a mold is made is never the same. A broken doll breaks more. When this happens you may be offered a low price by the mold maker for the doll. Or he may claim the break was already there. Your only choice is to take the doll. Don't let anyone make a mold of a doll body. Composition bodies disintegrate in the wet and heat of the plaster.

If nothing happens to the doll in the mold-making process, a crack may develop later. Heat from the chemical change in the plaster is hard on old bisque, causing cracking.

If your doll goes to auction after having been used for a mold, it will be listed as having the eyes replaced or reset. There may be some chips around the eyes from the mold-making process.

There may also be discoloration, usually on the cheeks. If there are lashes, teeth or sleep eyes, these are usually removed before the process begins. They could be lost.

To make a mold, the head is removed from the doll's body. The body is taken apart, then put back together again. It is like having a doll completely repaired, but no repairs are made. The doll's value decreases. We are apprehensive when our dolls go through this process.

If you are determined to let someone make a mold of your doll, have a contract drawn up. Have it signed by both parties and paid in full before sending the doll. An example of a contract is shown below. To protect yourself, you may want to have it reviewed by an attorney.

Inasmuch as _____ wishes to make a plaster mold of the head from my _____ doll No. ___, which mold will be reproduced to sell for a profit, I will for the following consideration, and with a personal guarantee for safety of the doll, grant permission.

Upon receipt of this signed contract and $___ (1/4 the current price of the doll), I will ship the doll. Within 1 month I will receive 2 completed molds, postage and insurance paid. If the doll is damaged in any way the borrower will pay without question the wholesale price of the doll which is $___ and return the doll. The doll will be returned within 4 weeks of the signing of this contract.

Signed _____

(both parties)

Selling for Profit

People buy dolls for speculation and investment all the time. At auction, dealers speculate on the dolls they buy, except dolls they put in their own collections. Dealers usually buy dolls that are less expensive, expecting a quick profit to cover the cost of better dolls. Collectors usually buy for long-term investment. Auction houses buy solely for speculation.

SELLING DOLLS

Dolls are like stocks—you usually have to hold them awhile before the price goes up. In 12 years of careful study, we haven't seen any group of dolls whose price has gone down. Often you can buy a doll today and make a profit by selling it tomorrow.

The value of the doll dictates the effort it takes to find a buyer. With a lovely baby doll, you can usually find a buyer the same day. When you get to a Jumeau, it may take longer to find a collector with enough money to buy it. Think about this when you choose a theme for your collection.

The size of a doll also makes a difference in how it sells. Often a cabinet-size doll, a doll under 16 inches, sells at a higher price than a large doll, even though large dolls still demand high prices. We purchased a 34-inch Simon and Halbig for $90 in 1972. In 1981, it was selling for $1,700 at auction.

Auctions will take one or two dolls, as well as collections. They also purchase outright, for

---

Bisque, French, Jumeau, marked *Déposé Tête Jumeau 3 Bte S.G.D.G. 4.*
The automation at left moves her head as music plays and tries to catch a butterfly in her net.

Bisque, 15 inches.
The black boy doll at top is wearing original clothes. He has painted eyes, a cloth body and a flange neck. Black dolls always bring a good price because they were made in limited quantity. The side-glancing eyes of this doll make him cute.

about 70% of the doll's estimated value. The auctioneer usually receives from 10% to 30% of the selling price.

Selling Many Dolls—If possible, sell a large collection in parts, especially if it is sold at auction. We sold 80 dolls at the end of a 3-day auction and we got a low price for them. If you have many dolls to sell, sell a few at a time. You can spread the profit over two or three years. The tax you pay will be smaller. Sometimes payment can be divided. For instance, half of the selling price of a doll collection could be paid to you in December and the other half in January. This could help with the taxes you must pay on your sale.

Some people take a table at a doll show to sell a lot of dolls. This is often profitable, but may take a couple of days' work at the table. When you sell dolls this way, have them in the best possible condition. They must appeal to the buyer. Set the prices at the highest price you want for the doll. A dealer will probably ask for a discount.

Often a doll dealer will buy 20 or more dolls from you and pay a better price than you can get from an auction. You will have less waiting and trouble if you sell this way. Doll dealers pay immediately, often in cash.

Selling One Doll—When you want to sell one doll, place an advertisement in local newspapers. If you don't mind shipping a doll, place ads in doll magazines, antique trade magazines and doll-collector publications. Most high-priced dolls are sold by word of mouth. When you decide to sell a doll, advertise it locally and tell your doll club. Know the price you want for your doll.

Donate To Charity—Dolls can be donated to charity and you will receive a receipt for the value of the doll. You determine the value. The value can be deducted as a charitable contribution. Churches will use your dolls in sales. Sometimes doll clubs can use them. Museums that handle dolls are also good recipients. Keep your purchase slip and a qualified appraisal if you do this. Sometimes a tax write-off at a high value can be almost as good as a sale, depending on your tax bracket.

Our Experiences—We have sold dolls through advertisements, auctions, doll shows and private sales. We feel the most profitable and satisfactory way is to sell to other collectors.

We have sold to and bought from many collectors and dealers. We did make a mistake when

Bisque, French, Jumeau, marked *Déposé, Tête Jumeau 5 BteSGDG.*
Lyric has blue paperweight eyes, an original costume and marked shoes. Her wool dress has deteriorated and the colors have faded. This is the most-complete Jumeau we have ever found.

we began collecting. A doll collector asked us to send her all our cloth dolls. She said she would put a current price on each and send us the money. So we sent her an uncut Gutsell, several other uncut old dolls, an Emma Adams and some Brownies. After months of letters and phone calls, we received a token payment. Don't send dolls to anyone without knowing what you will receive!

DOLL APPRAISALS

Doll appraisals are important if you intend to sell a doll. When preparing to sell a doll, do your homework first. Study current prices and check the doll for markings. If the price you are asking is outdated by even a year, increase it.

Appraisals and requests for appraisals are becoming more common. This is due to the rapid increase in doll prices. There are several reasons for requesting an appraisal of a doll or a collection. When a large collection accumulated over many years is to be sold, an appraisal must be done for insurance purposes. If dolls have been inherited and the new owner needs to

Bisque, German, 11-1/2 inches.
This unusual doll has blue sleep eyes and a smiling, open-closed mouth with teeth. She is a perfect cabinet size and was probably made by Kestner.

Bisque, German, 22 inches, marked *Special C.M. Bergman.*
She has an open mouth, two teeth, blue googly eyes and a spring-strung, composition body. She is wearing an antique pink-and-white cotton dress. Metal springs are used instead clastic to join composition body parts

know their marketable worth, an appraisal from a qualified person is the best course of action.

There are other reasons for doll appraisals. Owners of old collections, who haven't added new dolls in recent years, may wish to review current doll prices. A person with childhood dolls may wish to know the value of a collection to be left to a grandchild.

Dealers or auction houses appraise dolls. Dealers often consider an appraisal a chance to bid. They hope to get the collection, so they often appraise low. An auctioneer may appraise high, hoping you will be encouraged to put your doll up for auction. Auctioneers may also appraise low, hoping to buy the collection outright.

Prices for appraisals vary. Some dealers charge $2 for an oral appraisal of a doll if they are appraising dolls for other collectors at the same time. Some appraisers charge $10 for a written, signed statement. An appraiser may travel to appraise a whole collection. He will charge a fee, plus travel expenses. Dealers who do this hope to purchase the entire collection. Whatever you do, get a *qualified* opinion.

As you become more experienced, you can learn to do your own appraisals. These can be done even for insurance purposes. Use the latest price guides, the most recent auction catalogs and any other published lists of doll sales. From these you can come close to the value of your doll. If you have been out of doll collecting for awhile, it is better to have a qualified doll appraiser determine values.

If you are going to sell only one or two dolls, take them to a dealer or auction appraiser to get their current value. It may be unwise to sell to an appraiser. It is like letting him set his own price on your doll.

If you need money quickly, the best way to sell one doll or an entire collection is to go to an auction house. You will receive 70% of the doll's appraised value in cash.

Sometimes a doll owner does not realize there are two prices for a doll. A dealer or auction house usually buys the doll for about 30% less than the selling price. This allows for their profit. So, don't confuse *asking price* with *selling price*. Individuals or dealers can set or advertise a price for a doll—the *asking price*. This is only what they want, not necessarily the price they will get. Perhaps they will never sell the doll. The *selling price* of a doll is the price it sold for. It is closer to true value.

Always keep a record of the date and price you pay for a doll. Keep a list of increasing prices. For instance, our Hilda doll would have a price range like this over a period of years:

Hilda
Bought 1975: $300
Value   1978: $500   1979: $1,100   1981: $2,000

SECOND-HAND COLLECTING

A collection can be a financial help if all or part of the collection is sold to provide money for a particular reason. You can begin a collection for a child, grandchild or adult. Boys, as well as girls, can enjoy a doll collection. A doll collection could resemble a stock portfolio. It can be put together by the age of the collector.

- *Before Age 4*
  Cloth dolls, felt dolls or Madame Alexander dolls.
- *Age 4 to 9*
  Old composition dolls, such as Skippie or Dolly Dingle dolls, German bisque and boy dolls for boys.
- *Age 9 to 13*
  Bisque baby dolls, dollhouse dolls, wooden dolls such as Schoenhut and Joel Ellis for boys.
- *Age 13 to 19*
  At this time the child may have developed a taste for certain kinds of dolls, such as all-bisque or baby dolls. A boy may like wooden or wind-up dolls.
- *Age 19 and up*
  French bisque, if possible, or more dolls from a group the child prefers.

Dolls can be purchased and given to a child when he or she is ready to accept the responsibility for them. Appreciation must be developed. Some children are more responsible than others.

Some grandmothers hold dolls marked with a child's name until he or she is old enough to care for them. Keep a collection for a child or teach a responsible adult the difference between play dolls and collectors' dolls. It is wise to provide a dustproof case or cabinet for dolls to be kept in.

We have seen the results of collections started early for a child. One girl was artistically inclined. Through her early exposure to dolls, she made reproduction dolls to pay her way through college. She now teaches art, including doll making, and holds exhibits of her collection. Another young woman made a small museum of the dolls her mother had collected for her. She used the money to supplement her income. A third girl sold part of her collection to buy a home.

PACKING DOLLS FOR SHIPMENT

At some time, you may have to ship a doll. It is important to know how to pack a doll so it is safe. There are good packing materials to use for dolls. If you have to ship a doll, the best way is by registered mail, insured for full value. UPS and other package handlers will not insure valuable dolls.

When packing a doll for shipment, wrap the doll's hands separately with plastic foam or

Packing a doll for safe shipment isn't hard. Gather together newspaper, paper diapers, bubble paper, tape and boxes that are large enough. In this photo, we test Hilda to see if the box is large enough to hold her.

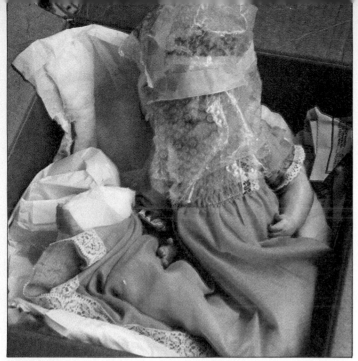

We wrapped Hilda's head with bubble paper and tape. Next, wrap hands and put tissue under the dress.

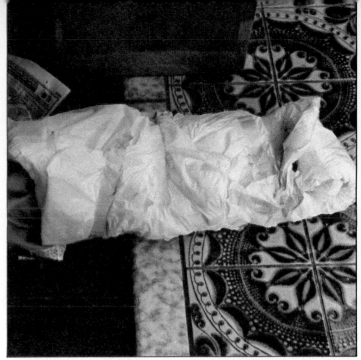

Completely wrap the doll in diapers and tape, as shown here.

Pack newspapers tightly around the doll. Have at least 3 inches of newspaper around the inside of the box. Tape every seam of the package with brown paper tape. Insure the package and mail by registered mail through the Post Office. Ask for a return receipt, so you are notified when the package is delivered.

bubble paper. Hold the foam or paper in place with a rubber band. Do the same to the feet, if they are breakable. Put lightly wadded tissue paper under the skirt and other parts of the clothing to prevent crushing. Remove any hat or bonnet.

Put a plastic bag over the doll to preserve its hairstyle and keep its clothes neat. Wrap paper diapers, plastic foam or bubble paper around the doll. Secure it with tape. Put plastic peanuts or styrofoam chips, bubble paper or wadded newspaper in the bottom of a box at least 6 inches longer and wider than the doll. This gives you 3 inches of packing space around the doll. Completely surround the doll with packing material. Put the lid on. Tape the box securely.

If it is possible, put the carton inside another carton with some space for wadded paper between them. This makes a secure package. Often the box must go without an outside box, but we have never had any breakage.

A box shipped by registered mail must be taped with *brown paper tape* all around it. The Post Office will stamp half-on and half-off the tape around the box to guarantee it is not opened in shipment. Boxes with plastic tape or other material will not be accepted.

If a doll is too long for a box or for regulations, two things can be done. You can pack the doll on her side, with legs doubled up, or remove her head and wrap it securely in bubble paper. The head can be put in a separate carton and placed in the box with the doll.

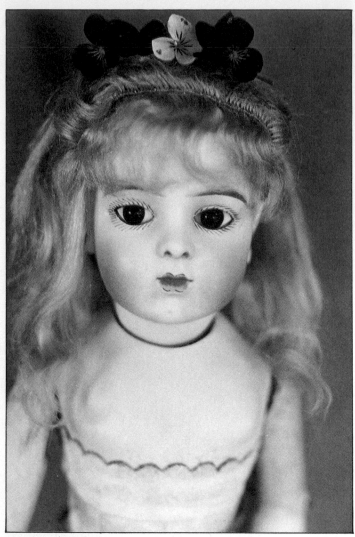

Bisque, French, Bru, 21 inches, marked *Bru Jne 7.*
This doll has an all-leather body, including feet. She is wearing her original wig.

The same doll wearing a bonnet.

DOLL COLLECTING IN THE FUTURE

There have been changes in doll collecting since 1970. A few years ago, it would have been difficult to get a collector to admit collecting dolls was an investment. People usually collected dolls for sentimental reasons.

Today, doll collecting is in its infancy. It is only since 1978 that there have been doll shows, doll auctions, doll magazines and doll stores carrying antique dolls only.

Dolls are big business. Some auction houses handle only dolls. Auctioneers want only good dolls and good collections. Auctions are held in large cities across the country. Absentee bidding is accepted from bidders all over the world. Formerly dolls went only to the people who could attend the auction with a lot of money to spend. Now buying dolls is open to anyone, anywhere.

Other changes have been made. Through publicity more people are aware of dolls and their artistic value. Since 1975, more books on dolls have been published than in the previous 75 years. Knowledge and identification of dolls are available to any interested individual.

Dolls are still collected for sentimental reasons. But more people are collecting them as art to be displayed in homes. While they decorate the home, their value is increasing. Collecting dolls for fun and investment becomes a way of life.

Index

7.516390428912